Always in positive mode

JOSÉ RODRIGUES

COPYRIGHT

For any information please contact:

José Rodrigues
hello@allpositivemode.com

www.allpositivemode.com
www.facebook.com/allpositivemode

TABLE OF CONTENTS

ACKNOWLEDGEMENTS

I believe that life is worth living depending on the amount of joy we can bring to ourselves, and to all around us.

This project is the result of a first step towards the release of my ideas about management, in general, and about team management, in particular. These ideas were consolidated over the past twenty years of professional experience, in contact with different realities and environments: in different companies, in the context of direct team leadership, in training environments, and also by taking part in teams of constructive debate in search for practical solutions.

Apart from the professional experience of every day's life, I learned a lot from various sources such as books, seminars, online sites, professional colleagues and friendly debates, that led me to important and profound reflections. I thank you all.

One big and special word to Mariana Figueiredo, ultra-reliable spelling and syntax checker. Thank you very much.

Sometimes, along my journey, I have sacrificed some family time in favor of my dedication to study.

We can rationalize a lot about the profitability of our professional activities, but this is not the most important thing to bring us joy. I found out that, if I want to bring joy to myself, I have to start by bringing joy to those people whom I love the most.

I thank my parents for everything they have given me: teaching, support and love.

The most important words of this book, go to my wife and to my children.

My wife was (and is) my best bet ever. She is the person to whom I owe a life built together.

Our children are the light and joy of my life.

I appreciate all the patience and understanding you have kindly given me.

1.0 GETTING STARTED

In our life, creation and management of positive contexts is an ongoing challenge.

When the human being is born, he or she has his or her full capacity in a latent state. The first moments of life are characterized mainly by observing everything that surrounds us, and by continuously learning without making value judgments.

Individual capacities of each person are developed gradually, with means to achieve various degrees of excellence. Those who are early provided with experiences that stimulate their higher capacities will eventually stand out earlier, as well. Those who realize that they have capabilities and enhance them further through work and dedication, reach even higher levels of performance.

Experiences are just experiences. Alone, they are not positive nor negative.

Experiences are only positive or negative when we value them as such.

Experiences are always considered positive when they surprise us, causing a sense of well-being.

EXCELLENCE implies SURPRISE!

Being excellent implies, necessarily, that one has the capacity to suprise others in a positive way.

The purpose of this book is to provide those responsible for managing an organization with the knowledge of a simple mechanism that is structured and methodical, which will allow them to enhance the creativity of their teams, since it is the only vehicle with the purpose of achieving Excellence.

Key Concepts

The quest for excellence is proposed through the systematic use of three key concepts by the company's leaders:
- Team
- Structured Information Support
- Focused Simplification

Each of these three concepts will now be briefly explained and further detailed in the following section.

In the end, evidence regarding the effectiveness of this method will be evaluated by the reader. It seeks to improve the general state of the company. This will have positive repercussions for both collective and individual levels that extend outside the organization; it is simply surprising!

Team

An organization of excellence must have the ability to move from the Collective to the Individual, and from the Individual to the Collective, whether it is inside of the organization or outside, taking into account surrounding relationships.

The human being develops an intimate bond between the rational and the emotional spheres.

Paying close attention to rational and emotional aspects is an ongoing challenge in today's world for professionals and companies of any industry.

TEAM	
RATIONAL	**EMOTIONAL**
Strategy	Communication
Structure	Commitment
Execution	Mutual Aid

Figure 1 - Team

In order to have a real team, we have to have a close and positive link between the rational and emotional aspects of the organization.

At the Rational level, the team must have a strategy to overcome every problem or difficulty. Without a strategy, the goal can only be achieved by chance.

After elaborating a strategy, it is necessary to define the structure that is required for the strategy to be implemented.

Finally, knowing **what to do** and **why should you do it** (strategy), knowing **who** is going to do it and **how**, we focus on its execution.

This execution addresses **how many** and **when** things will be done.

An organization that doesn't have the basic Rational levels implemented competently is an organization doomed to failure.

Nevertheless, the fact that a company has an adequate Rational performance in terms of Strategy and Structure, does not guarantee a good Execution by itself.

In addition to the technical skills that the performers who make up the structure need to have, (in order to beat the odds), excellent results can only be achieved with high emotional levels.

The strategy cannot be implemented if:
- Communication is deficient;
- The structure is not responsive and people are not committed to its pursuit;
- The structure presents lack of cohesion, is split into individual goals, and poorly wrapped together concerning collective objectives.

It is the combination of rational and emotional aspects that allows excellent performance with consistent long-term results to be obtained.

Objectively, the analysis of these six items regarding the performance of an organization allows for conclusions to be drawn.

The role of the analyst is to observe without making value judgments. Watch closely, looking to learn from everything you see, hear and feel, without making value judgments. Observe and record observations, cataloging them among the six crucial items.

In a company, the creation of a positive wave within the organization depends on the competence of those responsible for leading the team, and the way they are able to extend its activities to all employees, multiplying its positive effects several times.

"The boss only thinks about numbers!"

"Profit is the sole purpose of the company!"

How often do we hear these sentences inside organizations?

These situations are symptomatic of something that needs to be done.

The creation of a state of generalized positive spirit within an organization, presupposes the existence of a regular succession of surprisingly positive events for entities that are close to it: shareholders, employees, customers, suppliers, distributors and fans.

Whatever your activity, if you are motivated to achieve excellent performance, ask yourself:

1 - Do I have a strategy to achieve my goal?

2 - Do I dispose of an adequate structure to execute my strategy?

3 - Am I competent with the execution of actions that lead to the goal?

4 - Do I understand what needs to be done and why? Do I know how to do it and when? Do I know how many actions need to be developed to achieve the objective? Do I feel free to communicate my needs and difficulties with the right people?

5 - Am I really determined to succeed in this task?

6 - Do I realize that I'm part of something more important than me and I'm available to help and be helped to give my contribution to the common good?

Improve or do it differently?

The answer to these questions inevitably leads to a large objectivity on the aspects that need to be improved and the aspects that need to be changed.

When to give up?

The strategy defines the aim.

Usually, by answering the six questions above, we conclude that not everything is as we would like.

For instance, if by analyzing question "3" we conclude that we have operational shortcomings in the execution of a given task that is crucial to our success, we have to deepen the question: "Am I able, through training or continuous practice, to achieve the level of performance required?".

If you answer yes, deepen your reflection a little more: "If yes, what is the maximum time I accept for making such improvements and achieve the desired level of performance? Is it reasonable to assume that I can get it done on this period of time?"

If you answer yes, then commit yourself truly to the task!

If you answer no to any of these questions, then review your strategy and set other objectives to be achieved.

When do you give up?

You don't.

This is not about giving up. It is just about how to adapt your strategy to your greater capabilities, with objectivity, and only after thinking it through sufficiently.

For the team, the same issues arise. The team needs to get the same answers.

If you're responsible for an organization, you're responsible for creating and maintaining a positive wave within your organization.

A positive wave implies the existence of a strategy, a structure and an execution. In an organization where people communicate and perform their duties, commitment and mutual support are essential.

A positive wave inspires and surprises those who represent the organization. A positive wave radiates joy around and carries no value judgments.

Structured Information Support

Within an organization, relevant information relates to the intrinsic knowledge behind it. For the organization to function properly, its members have to meet each other, need to know the company's practices, rules of coexistence and operation, and finally, what are the local support resources if needed. To be an effective performer, each member has to meet the objectives of the organization, but also be able to communicate inside and outside the organization, as defined by the Board, and in harmony with the company's culture.

How can an employee have an intimate sense of well-being and a strong sense of belonging to the organization, if he doesn't know whom to approach in case he struggles to meet his/her objectives?

Pay attention to the dialogue between Miguel (Seller) and his superior:

Friday, 09h30

Seller – Chief, ABC's order was processed full of errors once again by the hands of "Production"!

Sales Director – Miguel, when was the order made?

Seller – On Tuesday, at 17.40. We are committed to deliver in 48 hours. Today is Friday and I'm not ready to deliver it because of the mistakes of "Production".

Sales Director – And what have you done to alleviate the situation? Have you called ABC to explain that the order is not ready because it was made late in the day on Tuesday? You have to tell them to make the order sooner!

Seller – Our company promises the delivery in 48 hours and fails! And you want me to call the customer to blame them for our delay!?...

Sales Director – Miguel, in what world do you live? A perfect world doesn't exist and mistakes happen. It's your task to make the client see that they also have responsibility over what happened.

Figure 2 - Dialogue

More often than not, companies generate unpleasant surprises by providing unexpected experiences, where the end result is a general feeling of malaise within the company.

Some organizations provide these experiences to their employees, their customers, their suppliers and, over time, their shareholders.

To ensure that the team is able to operate smoothly, the leader of the company has to ensure that there is an Structured Information Support that permits employees to communicate effectively and efficiently within the organization. This effectiveness implies that such communication can be successfully used in the pursuit of an objective. Efficiency, on the other hand, implies that communication is established with the least possible effort.

In general terms, we can subsume the constituent parts of a business into four major groups: Production, Distribution, Collection and Post-Sale.

Each of these four groups have their own internal constitution. For example, "Production" can be subdivided into "Purchases", "Warehouse", "Factory" and "Expedition".

Besides these, there are a number of areas of intervention present in any company, which are cut across all activities of the organization, such as: Audit, Human Resources, Legal Services, Accounting / Taxation, Logistics, Information Technology, Quality Control, Marketing and Finance.

We can define other areas within the organization, but the need for interaction between different departments will always be a constant necessity that every company leader has to consider.

Usually, problems are like snowballs. The more we let them roll... the bigger they become!

If an employee has a problem he can't solve by himself and has trouble finding its proper interlocutor within the organization, the inevitable tendency is that this problem will have major future consequences.

The effectiveness and efficiency of an organization are highly compromised in the absence of a mechanism of support that could be acting as a facilitator of communication within the company and, consequently, as a facilitator of individual performances.

This support can be arranged from simple observation of the activities undertaken by employees, and constituent departments. From here, we may identify basic information that is necessary for the execution of each task to be done as recommended by management.

Although it is widely accepted that this mechanism of support is essential for the proper functioning of a company, it rarely exists.

Companies have organigrams, manuals, marketing, procedure manuals, standards promptly disseminated to employees and instructions sent via email. Management believes that the information is always reaching its destination, and as such, it is considered employees' responsibility. Companies also produce internal training sessions, that are useful for clarifying aspects of the structure, but are often insufficient when the employee needs those skills and does not have the information he needs at once.

This dispersion of means, though useful for disclosing changes, is evil when you make use of the information, mainly because there are many consultation places and there is no single support which gathers all the necessary information, in an enlightening and practical way.

If you look at most companies, you will find out that their employees do not have a SIS (Structured Information Support), i.e., there's a lack of a clear and specific communication facilitator which could act as an operational support within the company.

Nowadays, we use our memory less and increasingly make use of support tools.

That is exactly what we do when we do a Google search and look for the answer we need in the options presented to us, with dizzying ease.

The construction of the SIS (Structured Information Support) is simple and based on the set of tasks performed by employees.

One obtains the compilation of all the information and fills a three-dimensional matrix with as many rows, columns and depths as necessary.

For instance, we may have the following organization:

	Production	Distribution	Collections	Post-Sale
Product line 1				
Product line 2				
Product line 3				
:				
:				
Product line N				

TRANSVERSAL	
Auditing	
Human resources	
Legal Services	
Accounting	
Logistics	
IT Department	
Quality	
Marketing	
Finances	

Figure 3 - Bidimensional table

For each cell, we define the required depth of information for each product line marketed and/or for cross departments throughout the company.

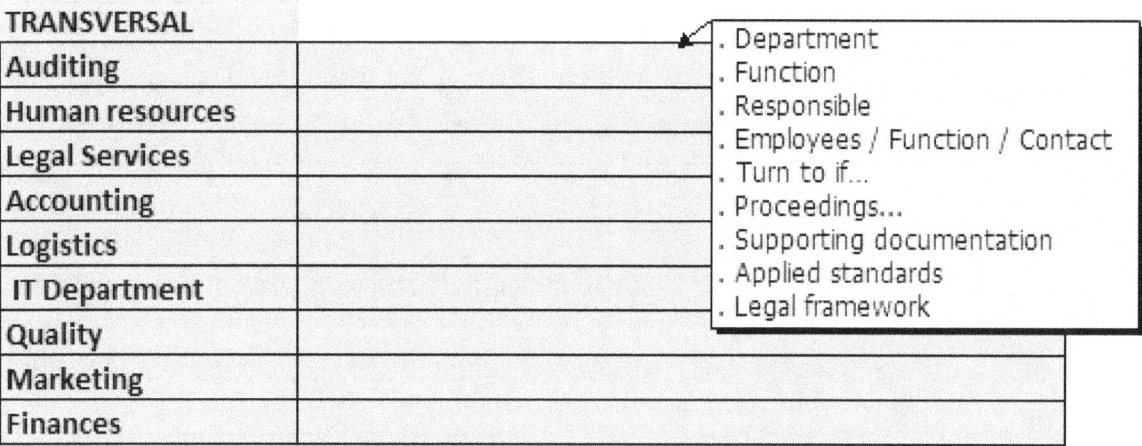

	Production	Distribution	Collections	Post-Sale
Product line 1				
Product line 2				
Product line 3				
:				
:				
Product line N				

TRANSVERSAL

Auditing	
Human resources	
Legal Services	
Accounting	
Logistics	
IT Department	
Quality	
Marketing	
Finances	

. Department
. Function
. Responsible
. Employees / Function / Contact
. Technical characteristics
. Sales Rhetorics
. Sales procedures
. Recovery procedures
. Post-sale procedures
. Raw material purshasing procedures
. Production procedures
. Supporting documentation
. Applied standards
. Delegated powers
. Legal framework

Figure 4 - Tridimensional table, 1

	Production	Distribution	Collections	Post-Sale
Product line 1				
Product line 2				
Product line 3				
:				
:				
Product line N				

TRANSVERSAL

Auditing	
Human resources	
Legal Services	
Accounting	
Logistics	
IT Department	
Quality	
Marketing	
Finances	

. Department
. Function
. Responsible
. Employees / Function / Contact
. Turn to if...
. Proceedings...
. Supporting documentation
. Applied standards
. Legal framework

Figure 5 - Tridimensional table, 2

Separating the information is crucial when dealing with marketed products, and particularly useful given the high discontinuity that products will suffer over time. What is sold today has little to do with the products that were sold five years ago. But many of those sold five years ago still require professional attention today.

What format should this SIS – Structured Information Support have?

Digital or paper? Centralized or decentralized?

The answer is in each company's practices.

You should chose as many formats as necessary in order to ensure employee access to information under all circumstances, so it will function as a foundation for effective communication within the company.

In the next chapter, we will expand on the essentials of this theme: construction, implementation, use and maintenance.

Focused Simplification

Focused Simplification is an engaging process of integration that brings people and constituent departments of an organization together, and it can be expected to yield productivity gains.

Productivity gains have four sources:
- Cost reduction;
- Greater operational efficiency;
- Greater innovation capacity;
- Higher excellence levels, i.e., a greater ability to positively surprise.

Why do people get involved and integrate an organization?

Herzberg and Maslow developed several studies that lead to understand the motivations of human beings.

Although these studies were conducted separately, both withdrew similar conclusions.

Human behavior is dictated by the pursuit of meeting their individual needs. These needs vary from person to person, either depending on their own situation (family, financial support, social status, etc.), or on their individual nature (areas of personal interest, talents, ambitions, etc.).

Generally speaking, we conclude that not all of us value, with the same degree of importance, certain motivational factors, although these can be seen as positive by each and everyone of us.

I understand that human behavior is dictated by its own Painting of Objectives, which consists of a Picture of Motivations, later framed within a Cultural Framework.

This approach allows us to observe different behaviors of people around us, with whom we interact with and without making value judgments. This implies using a perspective that focuses on understanding people first, and then be able to help or request help, with the highest degree of effectiveness.

PAINTING OF OBJECTIVES

PICTURE OF MOTIVATIONS

. Money
. Power
. Acknowledgment
. Personal fulfillment
. Security
. Pleasure
. Independence / Autonomy

CULTURAL FRAMEWORK

. What you believe

. Habits, practices and traditions

Figure 6 - Painting of objectives

In short, understanding the beliefs of people with whom we interact with, and understanding the reasons of their habits, practices and traditions is a key step in order to maximize their individual motivations for the benefit of the collective.

With the purpose of creating an engaging process of integration (of people and departments) that make up the organization, we need to move from the Individual to the Collective. This will also help understanding individual motivations of people who make up the organization, so that each individual contribution becomes important for everyone.

The Collective is the result of the established connection between individuals that constitute the organization.

If we wish to talk about this connection, we have to talk about proximity.

When we talk about proximity, we inevitably reach a smaller distance between people. Short distances result in a greater capacity for mutual understanding, implying a physical, rational and emotional connection.

A physical connection is established by the existence of a shorter distance between the parties (ease of communication and / or contact), and the existence of "ties" (e.g., an exclusive contract).

A rational connection is always consolidated by the presence of mutual interest in the relationship.

An emotional connection between the parties suggests there is genuine empathy, which is accompanied by a sense of greater understanding of individual acts and a stronger commitment to common objectives.

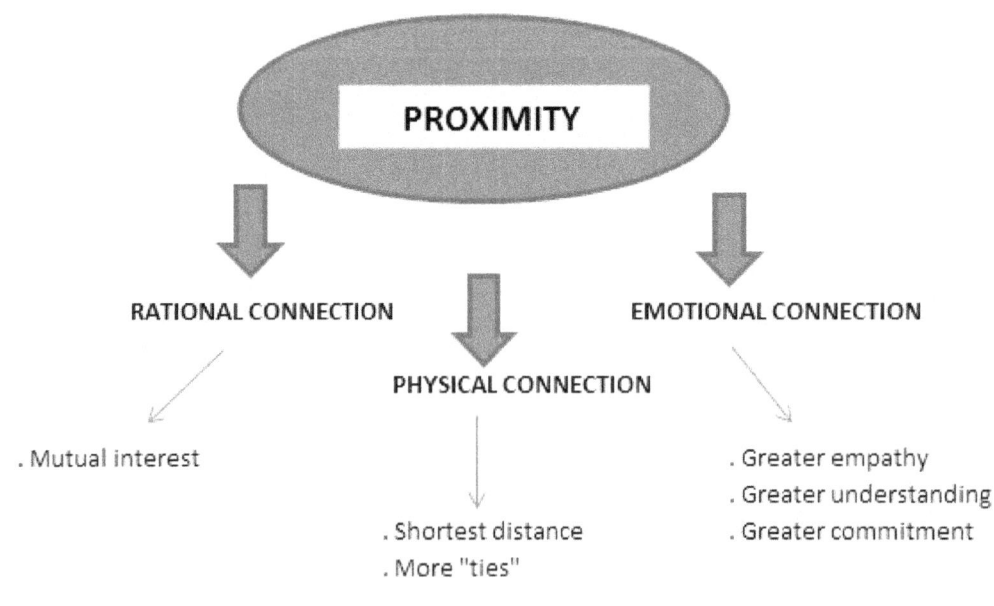

Figure 7 - Proximity

To create closeness and take advantage of it, is something that is made possible by the Focused Simplification process.

It is now important to understand the difference between a Simplification process and an Optimization process.

A few searches made possible to find the following definitions:

Simplification: Removal of bureaucratic obstacles of processes, procedures, routines or activities that generate unrelated flows in the processing of documents that do not add value to the service provided.

Optimization: Making a process faster.

Simplify: Making it simple or simpler. Making it less complicated. Reduce to lower terms.

Optimize: Giving the optimum yield to a machine, a company, an action, etc., creating the most favorable conditions or taking the best possible advantage.

The assumptions of the simplification processes are different from the assumptions of the optimization processes.

When we are predisposed to simplify, we assume that we can reduce the complexity of what we are doing.

When we are predisposed to optimize, our assumption is that we can increase production with what we are doing.

When the pharaohs built the pyramids, a way to optimize the production would be through whipping the workers, so that they would transport faster and heavier stones in greater numbers.

At the same time, a way to simplify production would be through inventing carriers with wheels that would allow pushing or pulling off large stones in large amounts.

Usually, simplification processes enclose a creative energy which is bigger than what happens in optimization processes.

It is by encouraging individual creativity of company employees for the common good that the organization is granted a higher chance of achieving an excellent performance and positively surprising those whom it relates to: customers, employees, suppliers, shareholders, etc.

For creativity to be effectively tapped by the leader of the company, companies must be oriented towards creativity, focusing on all relevant aspects of the organization.

In the next chapter, we will focus on how this process of Focused Simplification is built, implemented and how this development will allow the Rational and Emotional spheres to be joined within the organization, meeting many of the individual motivations, within a wide range, and finally, developing and maintaining a positive wave, that reaches all.

2.0 DEVELOPMENT

Team

Some authors advocate that the working group is only a team when all of its members waive their individual goals in favor of the group's objectives.

This approach errs by defect. It may be a symptom of group strength, but it is insufficient to guarantee the consistency of team performance over time.

The team is not stronger because the elements renounce to their individual goals; rather, it is solidified by rearranging individual priorities of each element.

The team is strengthened when the group members assume that the main factor of their satisfaction is that they are an important constituent of something greater than themselves. Consequently, their actions are to be guided by a desire to pursue the objectives of the group which are also one of their main individual goals.

No human being can renounce to his or her identity.

> **AMAZING**
>
> What humans can do when people decide to join forces!

The Team can be a diamond of brightness and togetherness when both needs, individual and collective, are achieved simultaneously.

The rational and emotional components are interdependent, and they determine the performance capacity of the organization.

We will dwell on these fundamental issues now. This is an invitation for reflection and for further deepening the knowledge that allows a working group to be transformed into a Team.

2.1 STRATEGY

Strategy

Strategy is one of the most repeated words in everyday life, and perhaps one of the most difficult concepts to gather consensus on its own meaning.

In its simplest form, answer the questions "Why?", "What?" Or "Why are you doing what?"

Strategy is the first element in the construction of the rational component of a team because this is where you define the purpose of the team, its raison d'être, its reason to act and its action plan.

By setting the reason of its constitution, the strategy determines the team's future. Afterwards, it helps to delineate the objectives that are planned to be achieved and the means to do it.

A team without a strategy is a working group that does not know how to use the resources at its disposal to achieve the desired objectives.

But the concept of strategy is deeper than what was noted above.

In the book "The Art of War", Sun Tzu advocated that military strategy must respect four fundamental principles: definition of the battle site, organization of available resources, implementation of measures to attack and contingency management.

Sun Tzu stated that "all men can see the tactics whereby I conquer, but what none can see is the strategy out of which great victories are achieved".

Tactics and strategy are often confused as a synonym but the reality is that tactics simply refer to the movement of resources (or the disposition of forces on the ground) and it is only a part of the strategy.

Sun Tzu determined immediately that strategic thinking precedes tactic development.

There are multiple definitions of strategy:

"Strategy is the pattern of objectives, purposes or goals, and major policies and plans to achieve those objectives, established in order to define what business the company is and the type of company that is or will be."   Learned, Christensen, Guth

"Strategy is a set of rules and decision-making in conditions of partial ignorance. Strategic decisions concern the relationship between the company and its ecosystem."   Ansoff

"Corporate strategy is the pattern of decisions in a company that determines and reveals its objectives, purposes or goals, produces the principal policies and plans for achieving those goals, and defines the range of business the company pursues, the kind of economic and human organization that is or intends to be, and the nature of economic and non-economic contribution it intends to make to its shareholders, employees, customers and communities."   Kenneth Andrews

"Strategy is a unified, comprehensive and integrated plan relating the strategic advantages with the challenges of the environment. It is designed to ensure that the basic objectives of the company are met."   Jauch and Glueck

"Competitive strategy are offensive or defensive actions, to create a defendable position in an industry, to successfully face the competitive forces, and thus, get a higher return on investment."   Michael Porter

"Strategy refers to the set of decision criteria chosen by the core strategic to orient the activities, in a decisive and durable way, and the configuration of the company."   Martinet

The term strategy becomes even more complex since its use has many embodiments. We can identify business strategy, market strategy, marketing strategy, human resources strategy, sales strategy, power strategy, environmental strategy and many others.

The fact is that the Strategy must come before any rational business decision, just as the decision precedes the action.

The leader of an organization must have its own definition of Strategy. Since I consider that simplification carries objectivity and helps the reader to reflect upon the concept, I leave my own definition of strategy:

"Strategy is the set of ideas and goals that ends up in the definition of an action plan."

Given this consideration, how can we determine whether an organization has a Strategy or not?

I consider that an organization has in fact a strategy when all of its elements are able to respond at once to the following questions:

- **Who are we?**
- **What do we want to achieve?**
- **What is the current situation?**
- **What is our plan?**

The answer to these questions by itself does not mean that there is an implemented strategy in the company, but if all elements respond in unison to these questions, it is quite revealing.

The answer to these questions allows us to foresee that all workers will answer affirmatively to the question: "Do you know why you do it?"

This also means that probably, the actions necessary to achieve the objectives are being set in motion, according to plan.

Both the analysis and the formulation of strategies have much to do with the environment in which they are intended to function. There are several schools of thought whose origin and strategic framework vary, depending on their reality, time and purpose.

Each organization has a specific internal reality that dictates how it draws up its data analysis and formulates its Strategy.

In strategy formulation, there are fundamental principles that must be present:
1- Profitable use of available resources;
2- Creation and seizing of opportunities;
3- Strengthening of survival.

It is of paramount importance for company leaders that they are aware that you cannot have a team without having a Strategy.

For the Team, the Strategy is the first rational element whose purpose is to align motivations, and providing articulation of actions.

> **Who are we?**
> Vision, Mission, Values
> Competencies, material resources
> Strengths, Weaknesses

Vision, Mission, Values

Nowadays, most companies present themselves to the world by announcing their "Vision", their "Mission" and their "Values".

Usually the term "Vision" refers to the way the company communicates how it would like to position itself in the future. The "Vision" is what the company believes to be its destiny!

It is widely understood the "Mission" is the reason why the company exists. Why and for what the organization does exist and what it is going to do.

The "Values" are announced as a set of principles, beliefs and orientations, that guide the organization. They are important for a successful implementation of the strategy. Values by themselves do not have a great significance. However, the values perceived by the employees, the customers, the suppliers and the shareholders, on the other hand, are the ones that determine how each person acts towards the organization. And those are the ones that must be present when the leadership of the company answers the key questions.

And here are the key questions: "Which values are assigned to us?", "Which values do we want to be assigned to us?". Those issues are crucial to create an emotional alignment within the organization. The answers to these questions are determinant for the company's culture.

Available resources

The first and most important feature to consider, are the skills. What is the company know-how?

The construction of the strategy has to take into account existing skills, latent skills and the potential skills.

The existing skills should be explored by the company's leadership in its fullness.

The latent skills should be considered, and nurtured, so that they can flourish.

Looking after the skills' potential, implies looking for skills that the organization does not possess, but that can be obtained outside, through by recruiting people, hiring services, or celebrating alliances and / or partnerships.

Finally, you must consider material resources, because they set the boundaries for the actions that can indeed be implemented by the organization.

Strengths, Weaknesses

Identification of an organization's strengths and weaknesses is an extremely comprehensive, complex and important topic.

Comprehensive because detecting strength or weakness points depend on individual perspectives. From a client's perspective, buying cheaper products can bring the advantage of the product at a low price and the disadvantage of the perception of a lower quality. In a financial perspective, the same company may have a weakness, which is a potentially lower volume of revenue (selling low) and a strength, such as a low cost production (lower quality).

The perception of the relative strength of a point depends directly of the perception on the relative strength of the element of comparison. It is here that one adds an element of complexity: the opponent.

Regardless of the perspective, the leadership of an organization has to identify its internal positioning in relation to the objectives which are idealized (strengths and weaknesses of current skills and available material resources), and its external positioning taking into account its opponents and the target customers (opportunities and threats).

Identifying the strengths and weaknesses of the company accurately and comprehensively are often an herculean task, but it is a line of strategic thinking that must be present in the organization under penalty of losing the ability to anticipate our opponent(s), and limiting our own ability to overcome obstacles or to be resilient before the customer.

What do we want to achieve?
Objectives to be achieved
When
In what quantity

What do we want to achieve?

Objectives to be achieved

Usually there is a multiplicity of objectives that companies aim to achieve with the actions they carry out.

The macro objectives, or core objectives, are the main targets of the company's actions and they can be of various kinds.

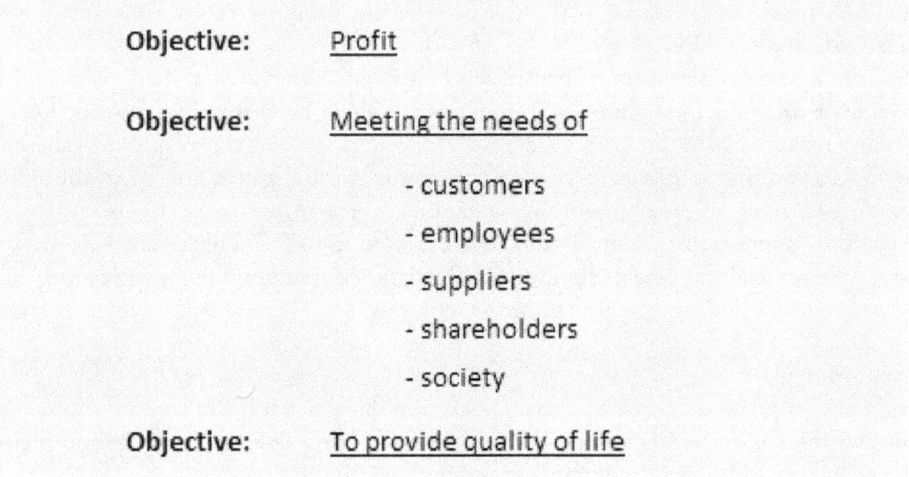

Objective: Profit

Objective: Meeting the needs of

- customers

- employees

- suppliers

- shareholders

- society

Objective: To provide quality of life

Figure 8 - Rational objectives

Knowing what we want to achieve is another step towards the formulation of the strategy. We have identified who we are. We now define what we want to obtain, and evaluate if our ambition is consistent with the capabilities that the organization has, either in terms of skills, or in terms of material resources available.

The more you walk down the stairs, in terms of objectives, the greater the leadership abilities to get together all staff focused on the main strategic objectives of the organization.

Knowing what we want is perhaps the most difficult task when leading a company.

Although it appears that we know what we want, this is not true the vast majority of the time we think about it.

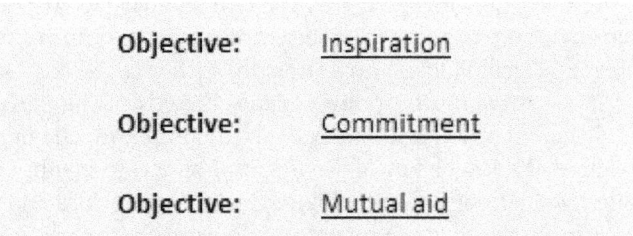

Objective: Inspiration

Objective: Commitment

Objective: Mutual aid

Figure 9 - Emotional objectives

The leader of an organization is often confronted with the need to combine the interests of different perspectives (perspectives of shareholders, customer insights, perspectives of employees and / or financial perspectives, business perspectives, technical perspectives, legal perspectives), and usually there is a tendency for the leader of the company to assign a personal preference to certain perspectives over others.

Finally, to worsen the difficulty, wanting to satisfy all perspectives simultaneously is something that will be as close to an illusion... as it is to success!

SOLUTION

Understand the problem.

Simplifying becomes particularly useful when we need to align strategic thinking.

If when we answer the question "Who are we?", we are aware of our vision, our values, our mission, our available resources and our strengths and weaknesses, it becomes easier to identify a core set of goals, which we consider achievable within a certain time.

Next, we identify the difficulties that arise when pursuing these key objectives, and seek to realize the cause of existence of these obstacles.

"Talent helps, but does not get us as far as ambition."   Paul Arden

To understand the problem is an essential step to find the solution.

An additional complexity has to do with the individual and collective breakthrough. When we define the next target, it is likely to be surpassed. If at first, we define a goal perceived as unachievable, it becomes even harder to achieve.

We must have the ambition to go further. We must have the ambition of climbing up to heaven, regardless of where it is located!

We must be willing to give our best to get there.

This implies working hard and competently. That also means we have to do so respecting our equilibrium and those around us.

By answering the question "What do we want: which objectives are to be achieved and when?", the leader of the organization will target the actions of all for the pursuit of these objectives within a certain time.

The obtained results are crucial and can serve as measure of the success of the organization.

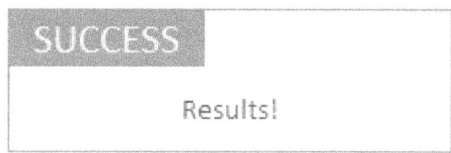

SUCCESS

Results!

Collective success will only be possible if every element of the organization perceives it as part of his individual success.

The results will provide the means for a Positive Wave to be implemented within the organization.

When? How much?

The definition of scheduled targets is crucial for managing the efforts of employees, monitoring activity trends over time, and to maintain a motivational drive.

Saying we are able to jump higher is insufficient to determine if we can jump over the wall.

Once the first wall is taken, it is a challenge to try and climb a higher one.

Once accepted, challenges are always a source of motivation for the entire organization. The real difficulty is to make each individual understand collective challenges and objectives as being part of his own responsibility.

After successfully completing this step, the next step is to promote mutual support among members of the organization in order for them to be able to achieve the proposed objectives.

"When and how much?" will have an adequate response, on the organization's part, only if they are defined up front.

> **What is the situation?**
> Leadership and focus
> Organization and method
> Contingency management

What's the situation?

Leadership and focus

We must understand the reality of the company, which is ever-evolving, on a daily basis.

The first look of the leader of the company should be on him/herself, and also on his/her management team.

Management involves four basic functions: planning, organizing, directing and motivating.

Considering these functions, is the company leadership the most effective it can be?

Is there a positive and immediate action by the employees in response to the stimuli provided by the company leadership?

What is the organizational climate?

What is the company culture?

The ability of the organization to implement a particular strategy is necessarily constrained by the capacity and urgency of taking action. With a more vertical organization, the leader of a company has greater difficulty to convey his message to all employees. In a company with a lighter weight and a horizontal organigram, the leader will be able to make his message go through employees more easily. The number of hierarchies within the firm limits the ability of the leader to act, and increases his or her difficulty to understand the focus of the organization and its strategic objectives.

The way the leader influences the entire organization is something that has to be considered when it comes to strategy formulation.

Articulating the elements of the organization together is relevant at the rational and emotional levels.

In a sentence, Frances Frei and Ann Morriss ("Uncommon Service" - How to Win by Putting Customers at The Core of Your Business "), highlight the importance of organizational culture.

> *"Culture doesn't just tell you what to do; it shows you how to think."*
>
> Frances Frei, Ann Morriss

The actions of the leader of the company must give continuity to the company's culture, and according to his assessment, he or she should realize which strategies may be the best answer concerning the path to be taken in the future.

How easily will the company's leadership announce a shift in strategy in case of need?

How easily will this strategic change be implemented?

Regardless of the organizational climate, existing organigram or corporate culture, it is important to answer these two questions because it is this response that allows one to target possible strategic options according to the organization's potential and current situation.

Organization and method

When we question the person responsible for a working group if he/she believes that they are organized and methodical, he/she will probably answer that it is safe to say so.

In the same organization, if we question an element from the hierarchy's base, he will probably say there are some deficiencies.

The man in charge should ask whether or not the activity of the company is founded on well-defined and methodical processes, comprehensive enough for people to be able to respond to the requests that may be submitted.

The employee who is at the bottom of the hierarchy should question whether or not the deficiencies that he identified in the organization are attributable solely to the leadership, or if there is something he can do to minimize the situation.

Responsibility for their individual performance is something everyone should experience. Everyone influences the organization's performance.

However, the role of planning and defining the strategic lines of business is the leader's responsibility.

Understanding if the company needs a deep intervention at the organization's internal level is another leadership responsibility.

The leader should check:

- Are the proposed objectives achieved on schedule?
- Are there complaints or suggestions for improvement? At what levels?
- Are there runtime errors? At what levels?
- Do the procedures have a well-defined sequence and an appropriate logic to fulfill their tasks?
- Do we detect undesirable situations (such as periods of downtime, overproduction, excess storage, failure of delivery, excess waste, etc.)?
- Do we see internal manifestations of displeasure or communication difficulties?
- Do we have the capacity to surprise positively, on a daily basis?
- Do we feel a general sense of well-being?

After this reflection, the leader can draw conclusions about the need for strategic intervention in the internal organization and eventually, redefinition of functions, processes and practices.

Contingency management

While building the strategy of the organization the ability to cope successfully with a set of possible adverse circumstances should be considered, while also ensuring it is possible to take full advantage of favorable circumstances that may arise.

We move into an important field of subjectivity, where the ability to identify critical success factors, is absolutely crucial for the leader.

While identifying critical success factors, the leader examines the possibilities, positioning and the relationships that exist, arise or change over time, because they determine the success of the company.

Depending on the nature of the business and / or activity of the organization, critical success factors have internal constraints (available funds, material resources, human resources, expertise, etc.), and external constraints (alliances with the competition, alliances between competitors, bargaining power with suppliers, legal frameworks, global economic situation, available markets, etc.).

This preliminary analysis will decisively influence the decision making process, with respect to actions that increase or limit the adaptability of the company.

Simultaneously, with proper communication inside the organization, members feel they are part of a structure that is prepared to face threats and opportunities that may arise from outside. Your own individual performance is an important part in the implementation of the actions necessary to succeed against competitors.

For instance, for a growing medium-sized company, it may be crucial to rent premises, rather than acquiring their own facilities. The rental of premises allows you to have a relatively low cost of adequacy of facilities to their future reality. If growth continues to be a reality, the company can simply rent other larger facilities and maintain their standards of service quality. On the other hand, if the business declines and it is verified that it has oversized installations for the current situation, the company should rent new smaller premises. In any case, the organization should be flexible in terms of cost control related to their physical facilities.

In sports, the man in charge must be able to prepare the team to play against opponents with different characteristics, in different environments, with favorable or adverse conditions, in each challenge. In business, needs are similar, and employees feel valued, individually and collectively but they also feel they are part of a strong structure, which is competent and competitive.

When the need to have Contingency Management is clear in the strategy, the Team is improved, either by the confidence you have placed in the leader, by self-confidence in their collective capacities, or by nurturing the sense of belonging of each element inside the organization.

What is our plan?

A methodology for planning projects by objectives

Balanced scorecard

Lean six sigma

What is our plan?

The development of strategic thinking is comparable to a river that will always flow into the definition of an action plan.

Thinking about important aspects of the organization, such as the identification of potential threats coming from outside, necessarily involves thinking about contingency actions. Even without a very elaborate plan, we can think of something such as: "if this happens, we will take measures to prevent it".

Any problem that is identified requires at least one action to be solved. Even other issues, solved a long time ago, call for monitoring to ensure that they were subdued.

The definition of a strategy is only complete when a plan consisting of objectives that are to be achieved is established: this includes quantified targets, actions to be taken and the schedule. Ideally, that would also include the assessment of plan development (monitoring and tracking) and of the people who are responsible for each action.

Each element of the organization should be able to answer the question "What is our plan?"

If an employee understands why he is performing a particular task, he will have a perception of its importance to the organization, and will also be able to adapt his behavior according to the collective interest. His individual energy will be benefit the common good in a well-targeted and structured way.

Therefore, the plan is the final element in the formulation of the Strategy.

It is the element that precedes its implementation.

There are several methods for the design of strategic plans.

Goal oriented project planning method

The GOPP (Goal oriented project planning methodology) is a detailed technique for elaboration of one or more plans of action to achieve clearly defined objectives.

This traditional approach assumes that there is a need for intervention at a given level.

In this context, the development of this technique is based on a simple model that consists of four sequential steps, as indicated below.

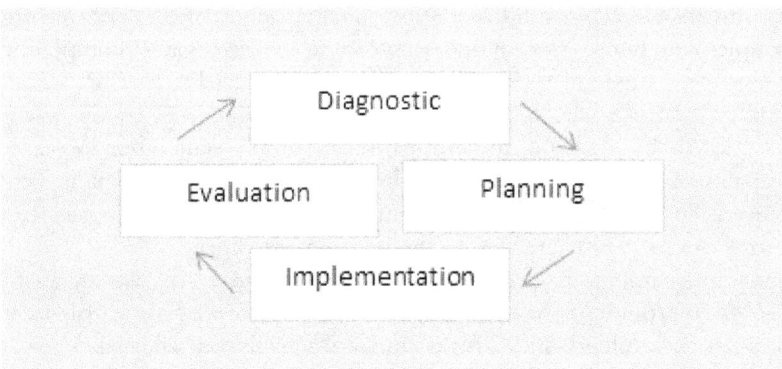

Figure 10 - GOPP steps

The GOPP produces six outputs that are important working tools:
- Problem tree;
- Objective tree;
- Table of measures;
- Table of Activities;
- Project planning matrix;
- Gantt diagram.

On the diagnosis stage, the problem tree and the objective tree will be constructed. Within this methodology, we seek to identify the root causes underlying a central problem.

This identification is achieved through various tools, such as questionnaires, interviews and observation.

We have to keep in mind some key aspects to maintain objectivity (regarding interpretation of data):

- Data may be skewed by circumstances at the time of collection;
- The three tools have different potentials: the interview allows you to explore reality; the questionnaire facilitates statistical treatment and the observation supports the collection of vast and varied information.

The analysis of suggestions and complaints can also provide additional information that may be important.

The first difficulty that inevitably arises at the stage of diagnosis is the fact that the problems are often presented by the employees based on the measures they perceive that should be implemented.

For instance, it is common for sellers to say "The problem is that our product is very expensive!", when the central issue would be that sales are below target, in this case.

Why are we selling so little?

It would be a problem that is necessary to explore.

We could be facing difficulties because the purchasing power of customers has decreased, or because the market is already flooded with similar products, or because competition sells cheaper with similar quality, or even because the product does not meet the needs of customers, etc.

Lowering the selling price of the product may or may not be an adequate measure to implement, but the selling price in itself and by itself is not a sales problem. Sales problems always appear if we get lower revenue than expected.

Constructing the problem tree is based on three steps:

- Finding out the central problem;
- Identifying other problems that contribute directly or indirectly to the central problem
- Identifying the root problems.

Problem formulation must be synthetic, concrete, and it must have a negative charge. It must be concrete because it cannot include suspicions, judgments or assumptions. It must have a negative charge so as to clearly identify a situation susceptible of improvement.

The logical construction of the problem tree requires that one should be careful to ensure that a given problem only contributes to one central problem.

We must ensure that the "central problem 1" results of "Problem 1.1" and "Problem 1.2" and once "Root problems 1.1.1, 1.1.2, 1.1.3 and 1.2.1, 1.2.2, 1.2.3 " are solved, the "Central problem 1" will also be solved.

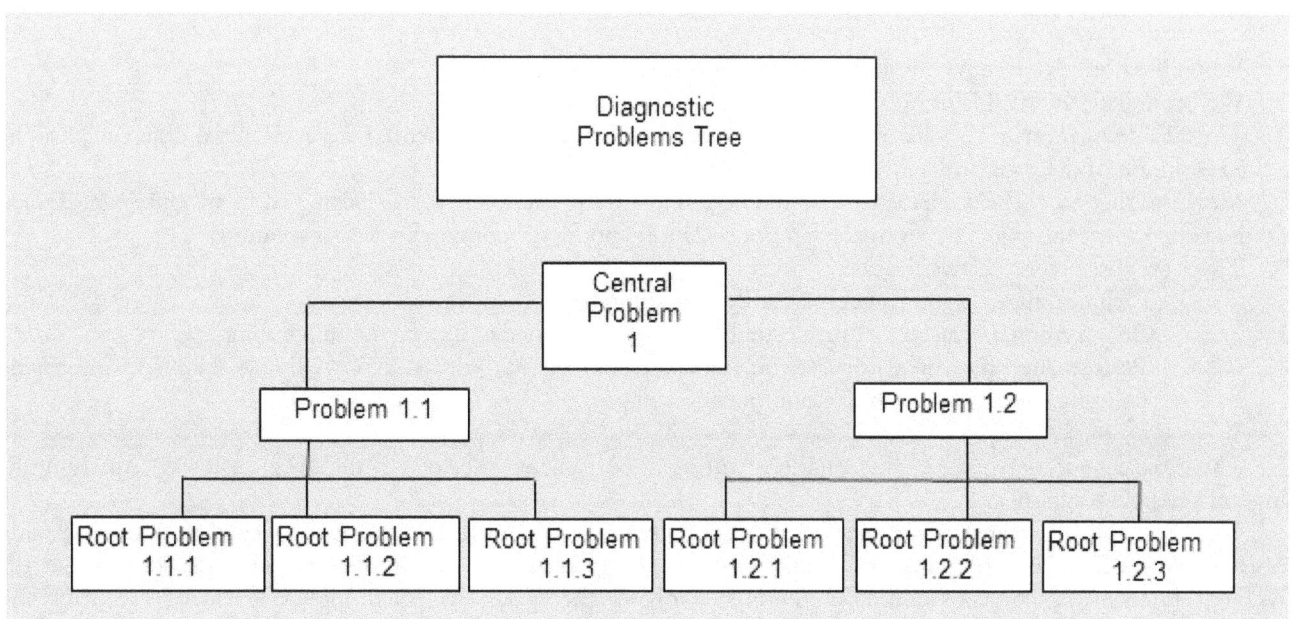

Figure 11 - Problems tree

The construction of the problem tree is extremely useful because the focus is on the root problems and thus, this makes us more objective and efficient while solving the problems that were detected. In addition, we will avoid resource wastage when trying to solve intermediate problems.

Identifying central problems also increases the objectivity of the manager, letting you concentrate on what is really important to the organization, and avoiding any distractions that may arise.

Once the problem tree is built, and root problems are identified, we start to think about how to solve these problems.

With this in mind, we begin by constructing the objective tree (next page) with specification of certain situations.

The key objectives are preceded by intermediate targets and objectives, and consequently, initial results have to be checked, so that the central objective is reached.

Initial objectives (objectives 3, 4, 5, 6, 7 and 8) will provide guidance so that one may find what the actions that will solve the root causes are and, afterwards, be able to help the team achieving the central objective.

In this example, objectives 1 and 2 are intermediate goals that result from measures taken in pursuance of the original objectives 3, 4, 5, 6, 7 and 8. The results, related to objectives 1 and 2, shall be measured to ensure the robustness of the solution that is being implemented.

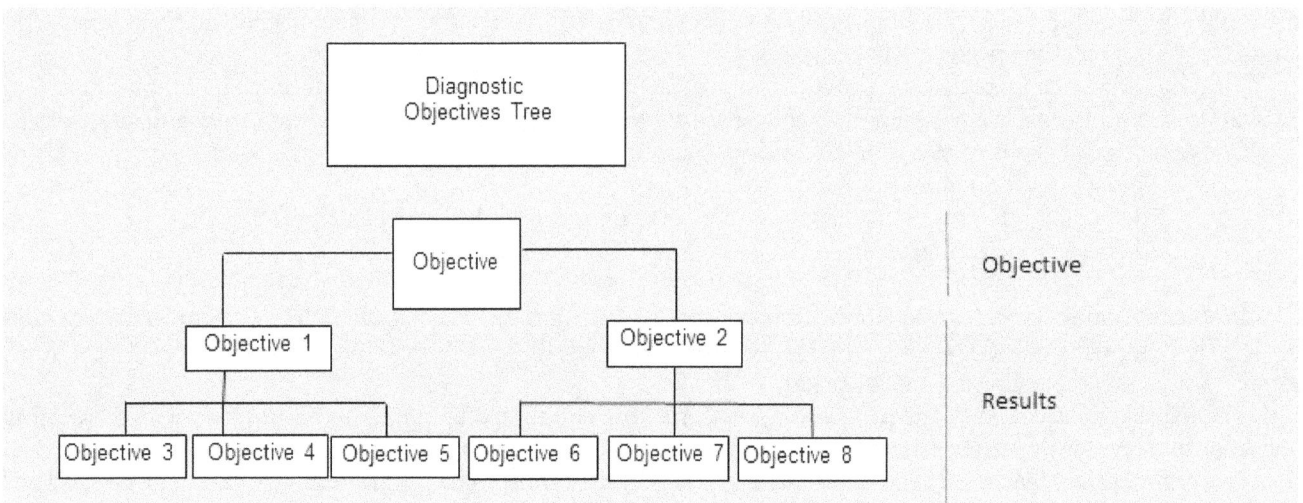

Figure 12 - Objectives tree

When the objective tree is complete, the stage of planning begins.

We begin with the "Table of measures".

The "Table of measures" will indicate which measures should be implemented for each initial objective, leading to the resolution of the root problems.

Measures that are to be implemented should be found among the workgroup, starting from an aggregate of ideas and dissecting them through analysis, making a pre-selection and finally coming up with a solution.

There are three types of measures:
- Technical measures, technical-scientific reasoning;
- Organizational measures of procedural character and aimed at improving functioning;
- Performance measures, focused on human resources, and aimed at developing skills and improving concentration indices and decision-making abilities.

The difference in perspectives that each element of the organization brings to the debate ends up enriching the range of possible solutions.

The leader of the organization must be able to influence the working group to focus on common objectives and improvements of the current situation. From here, everyone must proceed accordingly in order to devalue the divergent interests in favor of common interests, allowing the group to reach higher levels of creativity and commitment.

The measures are the solution that is found out by the organization.

Table of Measures

Measures	Problem 1	Problem 2	Problem 3	Problem 4	Problem 5	Problem 6
Placing of...	***					
Establishment of...		**	**			
Study on...		**			*	
Acquisition of...				***		
Training of...						**
...						**

*, **, *** Represent the importance of the measure to solve the problem

Figure 13 - Table of measures

The decision is made, so we have to take action:
- How can the measures be implemented?
- Who will do what?
- When will it be done?
- How much does it cost?

Setting up the "Table of activities" allows us to answer these questions.

This table can and should be enriched with information concerning expected results, actions and measures, and what are the constraints that may arise during its implementation.

First of all, the plan must be perceived as guiding script. Step by step, all participants will share the task of carrying out the measures that are necessary for the project to take shape under supervision.

Then the monitoring function should be understood. Everyone knows at what pace actions should be developed, and what intermediate results should be obtained.

At last, we must address the motivational component.

Here, there are positive motivational effects for the workgroup, whenever the plan is being fulfilled, and we run the risk of demotivating the group if the deadlines and / or the desired results are not being achieved according to plan.

In particular, the existence of the plan is always preferable to the absence of any guidance. If no plan exists, then the individual objectives of the organization members become their own motivational guidance. Each employee will act almost exclusively on the basis of their individual motivations, since they do not identify the collective goals.

If there is a plan, even though not being developed on time, it will continue to operate as an aggregating element. All employees can contribute to recover the time lost and / or adapt the plan to the new reality and also contribute to the unity and sense of belonging to the organization.

Table of Activities

Measures	Responsable	Participants	Time	Costs	Schedule
Measure 1	xyz	...		1500	Set - Nov
Action 1	jyk	...	2 h		Set
Action 2	qwe	...	2 h		Oct
Measure 2	xyz	...		2000	Set - Dec
Action 1	abc	...	3 h		Nov
...	...	...			

Figure 14 - Table of activities

At this stage, the organization has identified the steps/actions to be taken in order to implement each measure, and has defined how, when and at what cost they are to be implemented and who is going to do this implementation.

To finish the planning stage, you must be able to evaluate the effectiveness of each measure, and acquire the notion of the ultimate impact that may be possible to achieve with the implementation of the project.

In order to do this, indicators are set for each objective to be achieved. These indicators should be quantified (measurable), and dated (attainable).

The Project Planning Matrix must record the general information on how to monitor the plan. To deem it complete, it is indispensable to identify the assumptions necessary to accomplish the objectives. Thus, we are able to quickly identify any constraints that might arise during the implementation stage.

Project Planning Matrix

Objectives Hierarchy	Identifiers objectively identifiable	Means and sources of verification	Assumptions
1 - Goal	...	...	...
2 - Objective	...	...	...
3 - Resultads	...	...	...
4 - Measures or Activities	Budgeting Cost of measures	...	...

Figure 15 - Project planning matrix

Elaborating the Gantt Diagram to ensure normal and correct timing of activities is helpful.

Gantt Diagram

Measures	Set	Oct	Nov	Dec
Measure 1				
Action 1				
Action 2				
Measure 2				
Action 1				
...	...	...	...	...

Figure 16 - Gantt Diagram

Once the planning stage is finished, the organization is prepared to move on to the implementation stage.

In reality, there is no discontinuity between the evaluation phase and the implementation phase. Monitoring the implementation of the project will allow you to develop interim evaluations and, as already mentioned above, you can intervene and adapt the plan according to the contingencies that might appear, if these have been changing the assumptions on which the objectives and the measures were supported.

The GOPP (Goal Oriented Project Planning Methodology) may not be used actively and consciously within organizations, but it is a helpful way to highlight key concepts in the plan's design that need to be considered in the definition phase of the first rational element of building a team: the definition of Strategy.

Generally, any strategic plan notes five key stages:
- Analysis (framing, characterization and diagnosis);
- Principles and guidelines;
- Goals;
- Programming;
- Assessment (monitoring).

The GOPP allows us to have a sense of how we are taking care of each of these stages, and helps us communicate the strategy throughout the organization, both during its development as well as during its implementation, obtaining commitment from organizational members during the pursuit of collective goals.

The six outputs, which are GOPP working tools, help consolidate the actions of all and make the organization conscious of the need of taking contingency measures whenever the expected assumptions are not met.

The greater the involvement and participation of organization staff while setting up the plan, the greater its suitability, and the bigger their enthusiasm for the collective goals that are set. Consequently, the likelihood of a successful strategic plan is also greater.

Balanced scorecard

The BSC (Balanced scorecard) is a strategic management methodology that has evolved from a technical measurement and performance management.

The BSC focuses on execution.

When answering the question "What is our plan?", BSC (Balanced Scorecard) is different from GOPP (Goal Oriented Project Planning Methodology), because its focus is primarily on the response to "How much?" and "When?", leaving unanswered the question "How?". In GOPP, as we have seen, the organization identifies the actions to be implemented with a higher degree of detail and in the planning stage, this method gives a relatively good perception about the possibility of the plan's fulfillment. With the BSC, the emphasis is on directing the energies of the organization towards achievement of defined goals; it acts as a motivational and monitoring tool.

The BSC, as we shall see, has the merit of providing a simple output that can help raise the dynamism of the execution of the organizational strategy.

The BSC's basic model starts from the concepts of vision, mission and values of the organization ("Who we are"), and evolves to the definition of strategic guidelines, based on four key perspectives: shareholders' perspectives, customer's perspectives, process perspectives and learning / growth perspectives.

The definition of strategic principles from different perspectives is particularly useful within the organization, because different solutions to the same problem can be found. These solutions are often complementary to each other. It also permits that one establishes priorities while implementing the Strategy, maintaining a wide understanding within the company about the sequential order of company actions. This understanding often results in an alignment between people and structures, with higher levels of mutual support and commitment to achieve collective goals.

The prospect of shareholders is essentially a financial perspective: reducing costs and increasing revenues.

The customer perspective is confined almost exclusively to the identification of the target market and their needs.

The process perspective is directly linked to the structure, tools and internal organization that affect the level of execution.

Competencies, performance, organizational culture and climate are linked to the "learning and growth" perspective.

From the interaction between the four perspectives, strategies and their objectives can be defined, resulting in a map that summarizes what the company intends to achieve, within a certain time.

STRATEGY MAP

Strategy:	Internacionalization	
Financial Perspective	**Objective:** Achieve a share of 50.0% of total sales in the international market	
Customers' Perspective	. Reaching a 2% share in new countries in the next two years	. Introduction of two new products in the next two years
Internal Processes Perspective	. Consolidate 2 distributors of reference in the target countries	. Create a treasury department devoted to export markets
Learn / Growth Perspective	. Increase knowledge related to culture of the target countries	. Increase communication and listening skills of the sales force . Create a training and interpretation department for foreign languages

Figure 17 - BSC, Strategy map

The objectives define only the intentions of the organization.

To put these intentions into practice they have to be translated into effective action.

The BSC concept implies the development of indicators to measure the performance and the quantification of goals to achieve.

These indicators, when well-constructed, indicate what should be done to achieve strategic goals, and operate as a gauging measure for levels of the performance of each individual employee, and the whole organization.

Those are called KPIs (Key Performance Indicators).

There are different types of indicators and categories: volume produced/sold (output), production/cost ratio (efficiency), production per unit time (productivity), number of complaints (customer satisfaction), number of nonconformities (quality), objective fulfillment degree (effectiveness), number of expressions of satisfaction (excellence), etc.

The indicator does not describe the processes that were used.

It differs from the goal because the outcome of an action can be measured. The target differs from the indicator because it allows one to quantify the value to be achieved within the action, or set of actions, that are to be carried out.

The target of a KPI should be MARC, or M-measurable, A-attainable, R-relevant and C-controllable.

A KPI should be:

- Measurable, a good indicator that measures a performance degree of the organization or of an employee in due time;
- Attainable, because if it is perceived as unattainable or is in fact unattainable, it already works as a demotivating factor;
- Relevant, because the scope of the target that is set decisively contributes to the strategic objective of the organization;
- Controllable, because if it is not controlled by the organization and / or by the employees, it introduces a touch of randomness that can be perverse for the organization, by creating a false sense of success or when a good outcome is not the responsibility of the employee, or if you create a demotivating wave when the bad outcome is not an employee's responsibility.

The evaluation, based on KPIs, entails a set of difficulties. Often we have noted:
1- The employees remain indifferent when facing the imposition of targets to achieve;
2- Occurrence of outbreaks of tension between employees and hierarchies;
     i.   Demotivation;
     ii. Low performance as an effect of retaliation;
     iii. Manipulation of indicators (working towards statistics);
     iv. A measurement used to penalize poor performance;
3- Occurrence of competition between departments (instead of cooperation between them).

For the company, there are clear gains in objectivity by adopting this methodology. When properly implemented, it greatly increases the focus of the entire organization on achieving strategic objectives. For implementation to be effective, the leadership role in the company is crucial in three key steps:
1- Employees' involvement in the definition of strategic objectives grounded in different perspectives;
2- On the proper definition of indicators, targets and initiatives (actions) that lead to pursuing the objectives;
3- When the strategy is delivered, stressing out the importance of KPIs in aligning and motivating the entire organization in the fulfillment of the strategy.

Many companies associate the payment of productivity bonuses to the compliance levels of employees in multiple applied KPIs.

Thereby, the company is seeking to create a strong alignment between the entire organization, making the pursuit of strategic objectives an important job and a reward of all.

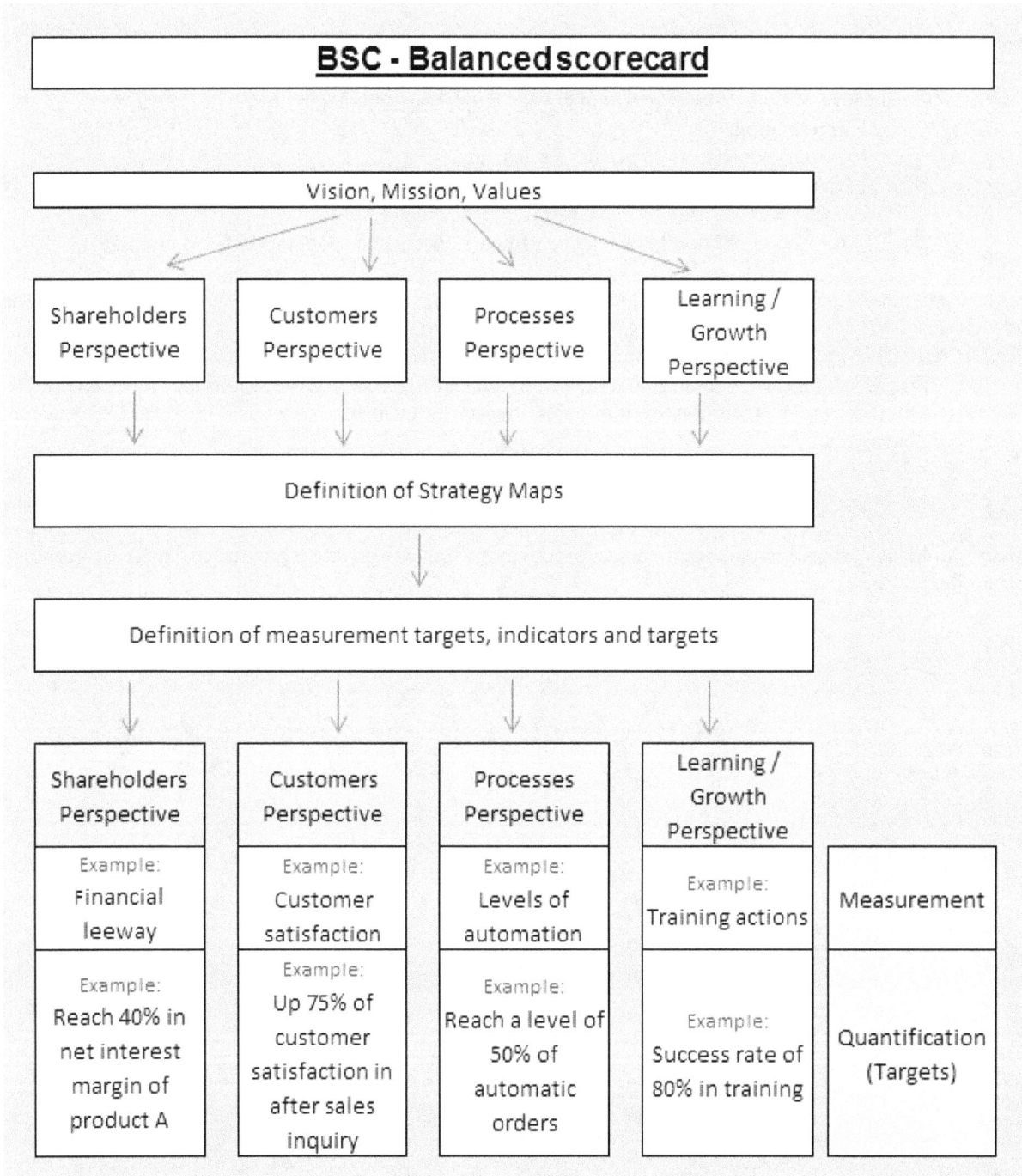

Figure 18 - BSC, General model

The BSC is a useful tool for tracking and monitoring the organization's performance. It contributes decisively to making sure that corrective actions taken by the company will be grounded on facts, instead of decisions based on hearsay, perceptions and / or guesses.

The GOPP defines the actions that the organization will develop to respond to the problems that were identified. The fulfillment of the plan becomes the motivational element of the whole organization.

With BSC, setting targets leads to better employee performance, because they will be focused on exceeding those targets. The BSC enables the organization to be resilient.

In response to the question "What is our plan?" the use of the BSC can be extremely useful, whether it is used separately or used in conjunction with the GOPP methodology.

By itself, the BSC is usually very focused on results and disregards the overall operability required to build those results.

Lean Six Sigma

The GOPP (Goal Oriented Project Planning Methodology) is a detailed technique of elaboration of one or more plans of action to achieve clearly defined objectives.

The BSC (Balanced Scorecard) can be seen as a structured quantification of the strategic objectives to be achieved, functioning as an instrument for monitoring the performance of the organization.

The Lean Six Sigma approach is an aggregate set of best management practices that are being successively and successfully adopted by several companies, of various sectors, at different moments of time.

When talking about the Lean Six Sigma strategy, we associate the objectives of these best management practices to the strategic objectives. This is done by adopting practices and philosophies of action that, ultimately, alter the culture of the organization.

Lean Six Sigma comes from the fusion of two techniques: "Lean" and "Six Sigma".

The Lean technique first appeared in Toyota, in the mid-twentieth century (50's - 60's). It aims to maximize customer value by rationalizing the use of resources (capital, human resources, materials, equipment and energy), and seeks to maximize resource value by reducing waste.

The Lean approach seeks the total absence of "fat" in the organization. It seeks to optimize the company as a whole, and not just the parts, of the production process. The focus is flow and speed!

The implementation conforms to the following rules:
- Analyzing the value chain in its entirety;
- Immediately eliminate work tasks that do not add value;
- Organizing work areas;
- Creating flows between operations and processes;
- Integrating quality into the production process;
- Reducing the number of shift changes, increasing flexibility;
- Optimizing the reliability and efficiency of equipment and facilities;
- Synchronizing production with demand, with low stock levels, and with shorts period of time between the beginning and the execution of a process (short lead time);
- Continuous improvement.

The Six Sigma approach has emerged in the late twentieth century (80's) in the company Motorola.

It puts the emphasis on the use of statistical tools to aid decision making and helps reducing process variability. It seeks to improve processes systematically by eliminating defects. The focus is on variability and quality!

Its implementation is based mainly on the following rules:
- Project selection is in line with organizational strategy;
- Linkage of the benefits of the projects to company financial reports;
- Connection of the project with recognition or merit system and employee rewards;
- Involvement of the leader and top management of the company in three key moments:
  - i) Financial commitment to the project;
  - ii) Active selection of projects in line with business strategy;
  - iii) Setting up tracking processes and project monitoring;
- Selection of employees that will be trained to lead a project's implementation;
- Identification and control of an "x" factor for variation of the result in the "y" process (DMAIC methodology);

DMAIC corresponds to:
  - D – Defining, it defines the "y" process;
  - M – Measuring, to identify the metric that is to be used, the measurement system and data collection;
  - A – Analyzing, for identifying the factors of variation and to assess the suitability of the process;
  - I – Implementing improvements, studying interactions between the main factors and optimizing processes;
  - C - Control, establishing control plans.

The Six Sigma approach owes its name to the statistical measure called standard deviation. The standard deviation is an indicator of the variation that we can expect around the mean of a random sample. The symbol used for the standard deviation is the Greek letter sigma, Ω.

The term Six Sigma results in the elimination of uncertainty, making sure that the number of produced parts, according to an average, is of over 99.99%.

Moreover, it eliminates the variability in results.

Imagine a customer who buys three times "x" parts of product "A" to the company "E1", having been informed that, on average, he could expect 5.0% of defective parts.

Indeed, placed orders indicated defects in certain parts: 8.0%, 5.0% and 3.0%, respectively.

The same customer goes to the company "E2" to get "y" parts of the product "A". This second company reports that, on average, he could expect 3.0% of defective parts.

In reality, he finds defective parts at 10.0%, 2.0% and 1.0%.

Does this client rely more on the company "E1" than the company "E2"?

The truth is that the customer can expect errors in any of the companies.

The Six Sigma approach aims to provide a positive experience to the customer by placing his or her three orders coming out without any defect in the purchased parts for three times in a row.

Ω	% Expected Defects	% Expected Success
0	100,00000%	0,00000%
1	69,00000%	31,00000%
2	30,80000%	69,20000%
3	6,68000%	93,32000%
4	0,62100%	99,37900%
5	0,02300%	99,97700%
6	0,00034%	99,99966%

Figure 19 - Lean six sigma, expectations

This approach advocates improvement and perfection of the production process until you get 3.4 errors per million parts produced.

Thus the company's credibility is imparted to the customer.

Hence, he or she is surprised positively and gets to know the connotation of "Excellent service".

The Lean Six Sigma approach is the sum of the previous two (Lean + Six Sigma).

It emerged in the late twentieth century in GE, General Electric, who in 1999 recorded gains of 1.5 billion dollars.

The Focus is on speed, quality and cost!

It is hard to be able to meet an objective without simultaneously improving another.

A process that produces too many defects can't maintain its normal production rate. Therefore, the process speed depends on its quality.

A process with too many tasks that add no value is more conducive to the occurrence of errors. Consequently, the reduction of resource waste (time, inventory, storage, etc.) contributes to improve the speed of the process and, by extension, the quality of the process

Faster and higher quality processes result in an immediate cost reduction!

Profit improvement is achieved by improving the speed and quality with which things are made.

Being only concerned for cost reduction without attending to the speed of the processes and the quality of its outputs, can undermine the credibility of the company, which will produce disastrous results for the organization's future.

Schematically, the Lean Six Sigma approach differs somewhat from GOPP (Goal Oriented Project Planning Methodology) and BSC (Balanced Scorecard). Strategic maps are delineated based on the Mission, Vision, Values and Positioning concepts.

The notion of positioning in the company can be crucial for the definition of the objectives to be achieved, and actions to be carried out. Although it is common that deep awareness of this reality does not exist, the company's positioning in the market and against the competition (benchmarking), determines the performance capacity of the entire organization and should be taken into consideration when developing strategic plans.

The market's positioning informs us about the important concept of segmentation.

We may have various forms of segmentation to consider. Two of them are the passive segmentation and the active segmentation.

Passive segmentation is the identification of market niches that add sets of customers with an identical profile of preferences (within these we can have separate operating segments).

Active segmentation consists in focusing on the customers of the niche market where we choose to be positioned, providing differential treatment to customers depending on the answer to the stimuli provided by us.

Within the same market niche, where we have chosen to act, we may have customers with the same profile of preferences, in general terms, but where size, profitability and proximity behaviors can be quite different between each other. Consequently, strategic thinking needs to take this reality into account, which results from the interaction between the organization and its markets. We come to terms with the fact that the actions of the organization have an impact on the reactions of their clients.

This is an important development to the extent that the organization understands that not only it has to observe customers, but also has to ponder how customers can respond to the provided stimuli and, this way, further enhances the positive effects of company decisions.

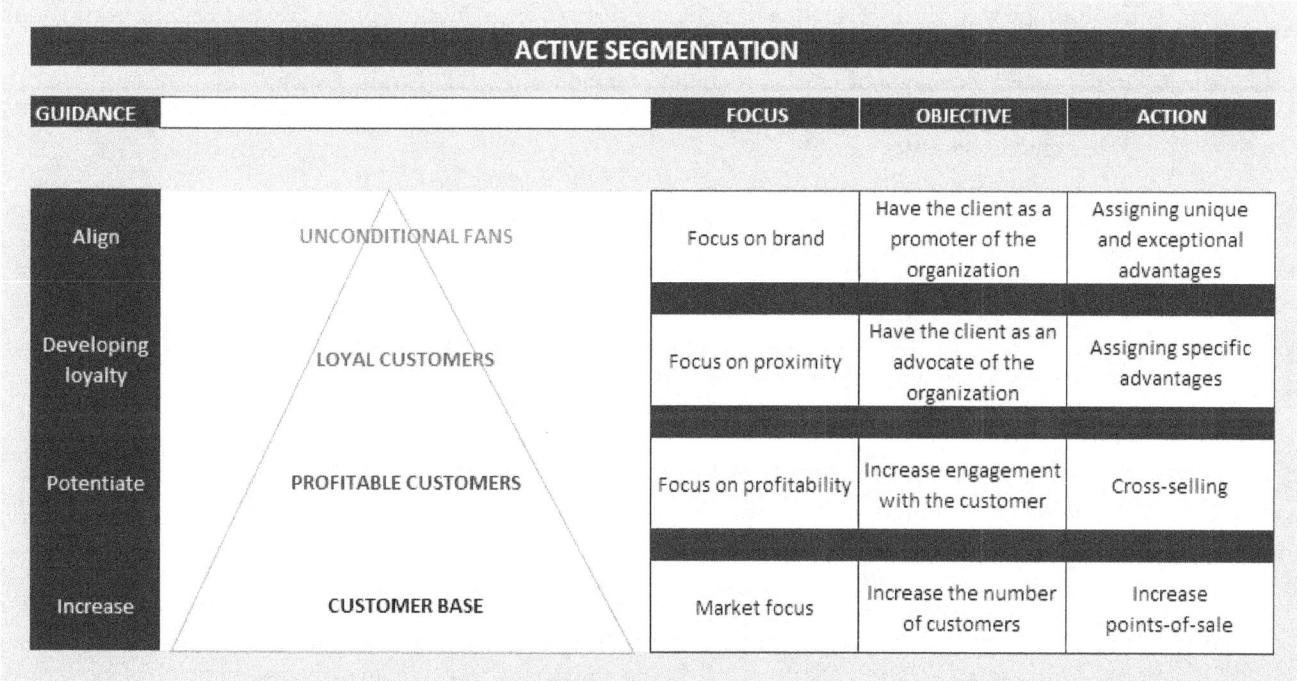

Figure 20 - Active segmentation

The organization can adapt its strategic positioning according to the circumstances it faces "upstream" (cost of raw materials, typology of suppliers, employee skills, equipment and technology available, etc.) and "downstream" (characteristics of different market niches where there are positioning and / or actions developed by competitors), seeking to identify the best internal practices to define a strategic positioning of success.

The first step of applying the Lean technique is the full analysis of the company's value chain.

This technique considers that there is a set of activities that do not add value to the final product in the light of the critical success factors defined by the market:

- Inspections;
- Packaging;
- Transport;
- Administrative activities;
- Support activities.

These activities must be analyzed profoundly by detailing maps of production flows in order to understand how they are taking part in the value chain and what changes can be introduced to reduce their impact on the final cost, adding immediate value to the organization.

Afterwards, we proceed to the analysis of the main sources of loss in his/her business:

- Overproduction, producing too much and / or ineffective production;
- Overstaffed, excess of time available for employees;
- Transportation excess;
- Storage excess;
- Excessive movement within production processes and / or between production processes;
- Excessive errors and / or defects.

The organization will then take action on these losses, streamlining the flow of materials, minimizing the transport efforts, simplifying the products' projects and process steps, standardizing work tasks and implementing devices that are Fail Proof.

The optimization of production processes will be achieved, obtaining significant gains in efficiency and reduction in results variability, with clear improvements in quality and greater efficiency in satisfying customer needs.

The integration of best management practices, throughout the twentieth century were successively adopted by successful companies such as:

- **Kanban**, by way of the technique of signaling that controls the flow of production or transportation in an industry, enabling timely ordering of parts, raw materials, transportation and other services, being an important technique of timely production methodology, JIT (Just in Time);
- **5 S**, a technique of organization of the workspace for maximizing effectiveness and efficiency. The "5 S" are mnemonics for:
- Sort (identification of the used items, leaving only the essential);
- Set in Order (To store according to the flow of use, from the most widely used for the less frequently used, to avoid errors and defects);
- Scrub (Systematic cleaning of items, ensuring the maintenance of proper operating conditions of the space, tools and materials);
- Standardize (Establishing standards for uniform procedures to promote interaction and / or exchange of operators, with the use of visual aids such as labels and checklists);
- Sustain (Ensure disciplined adherence to these rules and procedures, making of organizing the workspace a routine).
- **Kaizen**, implementation of a methodology of continuous improvement throughout the organization;
- Graphical analysis of process flows**;**
- **DMAIC Methodology** (see page 31);
- **Statistical process control**.

Statistical process control involves the definition, identification and / or creation of key process indicators (KPI's- key process indicators). These indicators will be an important tool for analysis and control of processes, allowing one to detect opportunities for improvement and consequently implement them.

These KPIs (Lean Six Sigma) differ from the KPIs identified in the methodology BSC (Balanced Scorecard).

In BSC, KPIs are key performance indicators.

While the Key Process Indicators relate to the registration and monitoring of events occurring in a production process, the Key Performance Indicators relate to the registration and monitoring of strategic results for the organization and are commonly used as an element of evaluation of employee performance.

The Lean Six Sigma approach starts from the definition of the strategic objectives and moves to the design of projects that will focus on strategy implementation.

Schematically, we have the following representation of the Lean Six Sigma approach:

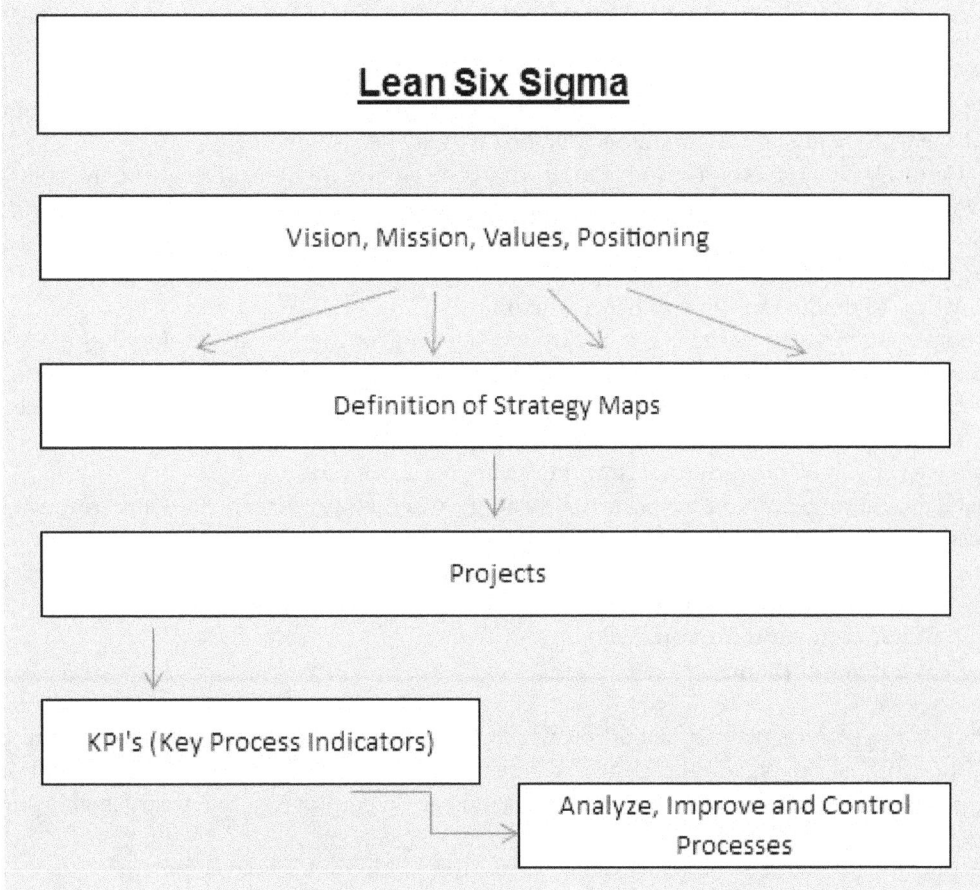

Figure 21 - Lean six sigma, general model

Final thoughts on strategy

As we have seen, the definition of the strategy always requires a profound forethought for multiple aspects.
Before you follow the important theoretical steps above, it is usually useful to ask yourself two simple questions:
        - What kind of space do we have?
        - Where is the energy?

What is the available space that exists on the market, the economy, the world? How is it filled?
What is the space our company occupies?
What is the space availability for our employees?
Where is the market energy? Where does it flow to?
Where is the energy of our staff directed to?
Place several sub-questions around these words: space and energy. You will identify aspects that can be decisive and that you would not do otherwise.
Life is the energy flowing in space. Each situation has certain particularities in terms of space and energy and the information collection based on this dichotomy, with no associated value judgments, often leads to serene wisdom and a greater decision-making capacity in the future.
Charging for customer self-service and / or reducing costs by increasing the services available may be counterintuitive options that are only considered when objects in question are looked at with a distant, unpretentious perspective.
Defining a strategy involves making choices.

McDonald's is an example of success in the food industry. This brand relies on its service model and a set of well-defined choices.

In any McDonald's in the world there is an awareness of what are good and bad practices; McDonald's serves tasty burgers with consistent quality. It offers easy accessibility, speed and service in an environment of relaxation.

Do you have to have lunch in 15 minutes? McDonald's may be a solution.

Do you want to leave home for a leisurely meal with your family? McDonald's may be the solution.

At McDonald's, the customer will get the food in cartons, eats with his/her hands and gets him/herself the napkins he needs. He will even be "asked" to clean the table he has just used and to place the waste in the proper garbage collection devices available for this purpose.

Are you willing to do the same in another restaurant?

These choices are strategic decisions. It is through our choices that we are positioning ourselves. It is through our choices that we are directing our energies into the space that we want to occupy.

It is fundamental to have this notion because people do not meet the same needs at the same time, in the same way.

Your own energy can be directed to occupy the space you choose to.

With that said, the organization has in fact a **strategy** when all its elements are able to quickly respond to the following questions:

> **- Who are we?**
> **- What do we want to achieve?**
> **- What is the current situation?**
> **- What is our plan?**

The depth of the plan or plans of action on which the organization will act depends on the complexity of the performance, the space of the organization, the dynamics that are subject to implementation and leaders' competence handling the planning, organizing, directing and motivating their employees' functions, in the pursuit of collective goals.

Creating a Positive Wave in a company begins, necessarily, with Strategy development.

As we have seen, there are multiple aspects to consider, and it is important to deepen the knowledge we have at the strategic planning level as much as possible.

In sum, regardless of the methods you use, or the complexity of the objective that has to be achieved, the communication of a plan is extremely important. This plan should be explained, accepted and involves all staff, lining up individual goals with organizational goals, is a key step to rationalize and align behaviors of all employees.

This is the first rational foundation of team building.

2.2 STRUCTURE

Structure

The structure refers to the body of the organization.

If we ask organization leaders if the corporate structures which they are responsible for are suitable for working, they will probably immediately reply that they consider them appropriate.

Since the Strategy is defined, we can focus on the Structure, which is a set consisting of people, resources and processes, that will enable the implementation of the action plan.

Sometimes the structure is confused with the organization skeleton.

An organigram can be considered the backbone of the organization.

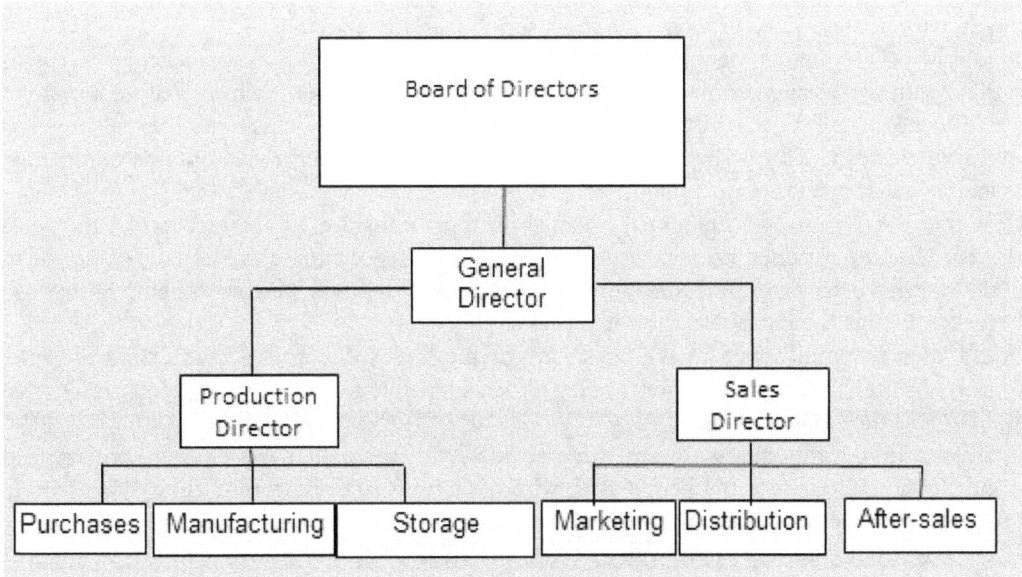

Figure 22 - Example of organigram

But the observation and analysis of an organization chart does not tell us much regarding skills, equipment, technology, information, processes and organization which people need to evolve in the company.

Besides the skeleton, it is necessary to understand and define the body of the organization

> ## Determinants of Structure
> Components
> Degrees of freedom
> Solidity

The intended structure, or the structure that is considered appropriate, depends on the analysis of its composition (people, resources and processes), but also on the degree of freedom with which to equip the team or organization, and on the hardness or stability that is considered suitable for the structure.

Components
People, Resources, Processes

People

People are the first and most important constituent element of the organization structure. Each person's skills or competencies are the first factors taking into account when analyzing the structure.

What can actually people do? What are the dominant behavioral characteristics?

A structure composed of a greater heterogeneity of skills tends to be better when facing adversities that the future can bring. In addition, it tends to be best for defining more diversified strategies in the present context. Usually, the union of people with different skills and perspectives leads the company to be able to ensure that each element will grow and develop their full potential within the organization, which is an important factor for learning and motivation.

Apart from having to bring the necessary skills for their roles, people have to be in adequate numbers for the performance of their duties.

The design of a functional organigram has to take into account the skills of the people who make up the organization. At first, it should be the organization that adapts to the people available and not the contrary, as it often occurs.

In times of crisis and high unemployment, responsible companies will eventually enjoy their ability to choose an adequate person with certain skills for a position in its functional organigram.

If the supply of competent people is limited in the employment market, insisting on maintaining a static organigram filled with the wrong people for the job is a mistake that leads to failure. People will not feel fulfilled and will not be able to positively surprise. Consequently, this organization may never reach excellence levels within reach of a competitor who does it. This is the kind of management that leads to the sale of large companies, and is also the kind of management that creates opportunities for buyers.

It is clear that the design of a functional organigram must consider, in abstract terms, the set of tasks that are necessary in order for the products to appear on the market, in negotiating conditions. The set of tasks which have been given do not have to determine the number of people who will perform them; rather, if these tasks are performed excellently, this is what is decisive for success.

We should keep our mind open to the possibility of the "Sales director" accumulating the role of "After-Sales Supervisor" and / or the "Director of Factory" being also responsible for "Purchasing Department" and / or consider other possibilities and their effectiveness.

People are the first component of a structure, so it is with them that we will get something done. If a given functional model is not suitable for the people with whom we want to do different things, then you need to conceive a new plan for replacing the organization's track to success.

People's skills should be evaluated with the utmost objectivity. Decisions should be made based on facts, avoiding decisions based on perceptions or assumptions.

In the late twentieth century, Billy Beane, at the time general manager of the American baseball team Oakland Athletics, was wildly successful working with a team centered around players that were forecasted to have a good performance, based on available statistics. He had built his team with a minimum budget and with players that had a low market price. He broke records.

The game has never been the same ever since.

Similar to what was done by Billy Beane, in any organization, the decisions concerning people should be based, as much as possible, on actual data.

First you need to gather the right people. Then you have to adjust the functions to the best skills they have demonstrated to have.

If you place Cristiano Ronaldo as goal keeper and Messi as central defender, what results can you hope to achieve?

Resources
Facilities, equipment, tools

The facility, where the company will conduct its activity, is an important decision factor that will condition the performance of the company over time.

The decision as to where the location of its facilities is going to be is never a short-term decision. Although the company can favor the option of rented spaces instead of purchasing a space outright in order to adapt its structure to their business evolution, the organization will always remain on its premises for a relatively long period of time.

Depending on the facilities' characteristics, the limits on the number of people who can work there, along with the type and number of devices that can be installed are linked to its capacity.

The facilities will also provide boundaries for the production maximum amounts that can be achieved through the available resources.

Installed equipment will facilitate the performance of different tasks that people have to carry out.

Facilities are installed, so the next decision concerns what equipment you should use. This involves an assessment of market supply and the available offers, deeming factors such as technology, effectiveness and price.

Technology determines the skills that employees who use the equipment must have, as well as the individual benefit they can get from its use, both in personal terms (comfort, for instance), or in productivity gains.

The effectiveness of the equipment determines its usefulness, because it must have a required minimum capacity that is essential to achieve maximum levels of production.

Regarding facilities and equipment, there are important considerations to take concerning their alignment with the strategy and the company's positioning.

The image that a customer has of a company may or may not be directly related to the image that is disseminated by its facilities. For a mail-order company, its physical facilities do not affect the image the customer has of the company. For a consulting firm it is quite different, since the physical facilities and the modernity of the equipment can establish a particular positive or negative perception in the minds of their customers.

While facilities and equipment considerations are almost exclusively physical and relatively static in time, the tools that are used assume a more dynamic role within the structure.

The tools used in the composition of the structure will allow people working on the facilities and with those devices, to perform certain tasks with more or less ease.

A tool should be seen as a facilitator of a final result.

Considering the tool's type and capacity implies focusing on the organization's creative process.

The computer is a device used by the organization (it's an element of the equipment).

Computer's software is a tool used by the organization.

Our company can hire people from the competition, who have been classified with excellent performance. The same people can work for us and presents us with lower performance, if our tools prove ineffective as facilitators of the final result that is intended.

The tools are the concrete component of structure that establishes a closer relationship with the Processes.

The resources that are important here, when defining and / or analyzing the organizational structure, are the facilities, equipment and tools because the remaining resources, such as raw materials and external services, will be equally available to our competition.

The tools that we use allow for subtle gains in productivity that can translate into bigger gains in competitiveness.

An organization that has greater capacity for processing information, will acquire productivity gains, crucial to overcome the competition.

Currently, computer tools play a differentiating role, which is very important and fundamental to any activity.

Pay attention to the examples given below:
1- Prioritize the treatment of orders that are more valuable;
2- Signaling and controlling debt collections.

1- Prioritize the treatment of orders that are more valuable

Usually, companies are organized around a FIFO system (Firt in, first out - First in, First out), in which the orders are handled sequentially as they arrive to the company, without taking into account differences in value that each order may represent.

Instead of using a FIFO system, the company can improve the overall results, by opting to prioritize higher value orders and processing them first, at the expense of low value orders.

Obviously, one should not neglect any order.

But one can and should create rules, procedures and mechanisms which expedite the processing of higher volume orders and maintain treatment of lower value requests at satisfactory levels.

With the aid of software tools, these kinds of systems are now easy to implement.

By giving a priority treatment to orders of greater value, the company is contributing greatly to the accumulation of better results in the shortest amount of time.

There is also an increase in efficiency. The obtained results will get employees enthusiastic. Enthusiasm is contagious and positive to everyone who is moved by the organization.

2- Signaling and controlling debt collections.

If we are faced with a strictly for-profit organization, controlling recoveries assumes greater relevance.

More than having a group of employees dedicated to control customers' cash receipts, it would be great if we could create a mechanism of automatic alert for customers themselves, inducing in them this good practice in order for them to comply timely with their commitments.

If customers can view their current account through electronic means (digital extract, query via website, email, etc.), we can create a simple signaling mechanism for the evolution of their bills over the past twelve months.

Imagine that Company XYZ is our customer, and that they intend to settle their bills within 60 days after order placement.

When we design a tool to aid debt management, we often limit ourselves to a form of query that mirrors the indication of the balance that is owed and its origin.

In this case, for checking its balance, the company sees the following information:

Client	XYZ Lda		Date	15-03-2014
			Balance	105.077,00

Order	Date	Invoice	Amount	Days
20140014	03-01-2014	12345	12.534,00	71
20140015	08-01-2014	12546	8.754,00	66
20140016	07-02-2014	12768	23.789,00	36
20140017	15-03-2014	12987	60.000,00	0

Figure 23 - Mechanism of controlling debt collections, 1

We now know that the company owes us 105.077,00 €.

A closer examination shows that the company has some invoices overdue, although they are not a very large amount taking into account the total debt.

We can improve this information so that our debt collection department can act effectively, asking the client for the correct value that should have already been received.

We could have improved this tool like this:

Client	XYZ Lda		Date	15-03-2014
			Balance	105.077,00
			+ 60 days	21.288,00

Order	Date	Invoice	Amount	Days
20140014	03-01-2014	12345	12.534,00	71
20140015	08-01-2014	12546	8.754,00	66
20140016	07-02-2014	12768	23.789,00	36
20140017	15-03-2014	12987	60.000,00	0

Figure 24 - Mechanism of controlling debt collections, 2

At this time we know exactly, and at first glance, that the debt of company XYZ that is overdue amounts to € 21,288.00, and we are able to contact them in order to settle this value.

Even though customer debt is superior to that amount, only this value is due.

However, this improvement of our tool helps us get a more effective control over the debt collection, and minimizes the need for explanations to the client at the time we contacted them to reclaim the value(s) out of date.

Yet, this software tool does not influence the client to be preoccupied with meeting the deadlines (60 days in this example).

Client	XYZ Lda		Date	15-03-2014
			Balance	105.077,00
	F M A M J J A S O N D J		+ 60 days	21.288,00
	√ √ √ √√√ √√ √ √ √X			

Order	Date	Invoice	Amount	Days
20140014	03-01-2014	12345	12.534,00	71
20140015	08-01-2014	12546	8.754,00	66
20140016	07-02-2014	12768	23.789,00	36
20140017	15-03-2014	12987	60.000,00	0

Figure 25 - Mechanism of controlling debt collections, 3

We may introduce the information that exists in the organization, but is not being used at the moment.

We can, for example, add a monthly sign concerning charges' progression in the last twelve months. Whenever orders are not settled in a given month, within 60 days, this month will be flagged with a red "X". Whenever orders are settled in a timely manner, the month will be flagged with the green sign "√".

This time, the tool is a great help for managing collections. For us, besides telling us that there is € 21,288.00 in arrears of € 105,077.00 that company XYZ owes us, it also tells us that this is the first time in the last 12 months that the customer records a default.

"We cannot do great things, only small things with great love."

Madre Teresa of Calcutta

When the collections department contacts the client to claim the amount, it can inform the client immediately that we are aware that the company was always dutiful, until now. However, this is value we are requesting to be corrected.

This is helpful for company XYZ, as with no contact whatsoever from our collections department, they will now be careful not to be late for any month so they do not end up getting any red record in its history. With this tool, we can influence the customer's behavior which benefits us both. This tool creates a competitive advantage over competitors. In case of financial difficulties, it is possible that company XYZ is inclined to settle the debts to our company first, before doing that with another supplier that does not have this monitoring mechanism. Besides what was been said above, this tool also provides additional information: it can tell us immediately if company XYZ is a regular customer.

Client	XYZ Lda		Date	15-03-2014
			Balance	105.077,00
	F M A M J J A S O N D J		+ 60 days	21.288,00

Order	Date	Invoice	Amount	Days
20140014	03-01-2014	12345	12.534,00	71
20140015	08-01-2014	12546	8.754,00	66
20140016	07-02-2014	12768	23.789,00	36
20140017	15-03-2014	12987	60.000,00	0

Figure 26 - Mechanism of controlling debt collections, 4

Months marked with a black ball were times when the company did not place any orders. By using this tool we immediately realize that the customer owes us a lot of money, that the customer has an overdue debt, but that they usually meet the payments when they are due and how often they place orders…

Now compare with the original tool and point out which one is the most effective for helping us manage customer payments.

It includes just a few more efforts in terms of computer programming, allowing us to get huge productivity gains, improve the quality of what we do daily, and facilitate the achievement of results, using the same information that we already have available in our organization.

Concerning resources in the organizational structure, information processing tools are a critical success factor. They are of paramount importance if you want to outperform the competition and to raise your performance levels!

Software tools are an example of how we should pay attention to the tools we use. All the tools used by the organization must be considered when analyzing the Structure.

Processes
Rules, flows, timing

After people and resources, processes are the third component of Structure.
There is a lot to say regarding the definition of production processes.
These should be as simple as possible with regard to rules and operational flows.

The main consideration to take when defining rules is looking out for the behavior they might induce. It is extremely important that rules promote positive behaviors and should not function as inhibitors of the behavior and / or as promoters of perverse effects.

Let's see.

Imagine a law firm that works with real estate and usually makes three-year contracts with its clients. Let's assume that this firm has the following rule for their negotiations:

"To face competition, the commercialization of new contract at less than what we have done so far is allowed, and we are accepting negotiations between 6,000.00 and 12,000.00 euros for annual prices. For contracts which are in progress, there will be no annual price revision".

In light of this rule, when employees are face to face with a potential customer, they will have a tremendous incentive to negotiate the contract for the low price of € 6000.00 a year, when the interest of the company is to celebrate contracts at the highest possible price.

This impediment to revise the contract price in the course of negotiations will make negotiators increasingly cautious: they will sell for a lower price immediately, because they know that if a customer disputes the price in the future, they will not have any leeway for holding the client.

If an organization's representative is aware that he or she has room for negotiating the price of the contract with the customer today but also in the near future, he or she will seek to establish an effective trading at the highest price that he or she can get, at all times. His/her focus will be on the contract's profitability.

Being aware that one cannot revise the price in the future, one will be conducting negotiations focusing on maintaining that same contract.

Imagine this: the contract has not been established yet, and already your employee fears losing it.

This situation is a good example of how the established rules can have perverse effects, i.e., they can stimulate practices that do not support the best interests of the organization.

Every organization has its own rules. These rules must be adapted to other components of the structure.

Every production activity has a set of tasks carried out to obtain the final product.

Like rules, the flows established within activities are of utmost importance.

Also, on this level, it is important to understand and analyze what are the best practices in the organization.

The 5S methodology addressed in the Lean strategy (or Lean Six Sigma) provides us a good example.

This is a methodology that evolves linearity.

» Sorting
    » Simplifying
        » Systematic cleaning
            » Standardizing
                » Sustaining

It can evolve profoundly with each item.

In the next table, each item positively evolves over five levels:

1- Just starting;
2- Focus on the basics;
3- Make it visual;
4- Focus on reliability;
5- Continuously improve.

These five steps can effectively be applied over any process.

It is necessary to go through a period of evolution to achieve the stage of development that allows us to focus on continuous improvement.

The simplicity of processes often provides productivity gains and effectiveness by reducing execution errors.

5S Levels of Achievement				
Level 5: Continuously Improve	Cleanliness problems are identified and mess prevention actions are in place.	Items that are needed can be retrieved in 30 seconds and require a minimum number of steps.	Potential problems are identified and counter measures are documented.	Reliable methods and standards for housekeeping, daily inspections and workspace arrangement are shared and are used throughout similar work areas.	Root problems are eliminated and improvement actions focus on developing preventive methods.
Level 4: Focus on Reliability	Working areas have documented housekeeping responsabilities and shedules and the assignments are consistently followed.	Items that are needed in working areas are minimized in number and are properly arranged for use and retrieval.	Inspection occurs during daily cleaning of working areas, equipment and supplies.	Reliable methods and standards for housekeeping, daily inspections and workplace arrangement are documented and followed by all members of the work group.	Sources and frequency of problems are documented as part of routine work, root problems are identified, and corrective action plans are developed.
Level 3: Make It Visual	Initial cleaning has been performed and sources of spills and messes are identified and corrected.	Items that are needed are outlined , dedicated locations are properly labeled and quantities are determined.	Visual controls and identifiers are established and marked for the working areas, equipment, files and supplies.	Working group has documented agreements on visual controls, labeling of itens, and required quantities of needed itens.	Working group is routinely checking their working area to maintain 5S agreements.
Level 2: Focus on Basics	Itens that are needed/not needed are identified. Those not needed are removed from work area.	Itens that are needed are safely stored and organized according to frequency of use.	Key working area items to be checked are identified and acceptable performance levels documented.	Working group has documented agreements for needed itens, organization and work area controls.	Initial 5S level has been determined, and performance is documented and posted in working areas.
Level 1: Just Beginning	Itens that are needed/not needed are mixed throughout the work area.	Itens are placed randomly throughout the workspace.	Key working area items to be checked are not identified and are unmarked.	Working area methods are not consistently followed and are undocumented.	Checking working areas is randomly performed and there is no visual measurement of 5S.
Place the yellow box where each one of your working areas are on the 5S Levels of Achievement	**Sorting**	**Simplifying**	**Systematic cleaning**	**Standardizing**	**Sustaining**
Fonte: reliabilityweb.com					

Figure 27 - 5S, levels of achievement

By deepening our reflection over several aspects related to a company's organization, we managed to get greater objectivity in relation to what are the necessary actions to promote an improved quality of life for all.

The vision provided in the table above is crucial, for it shows where we are and defines where we want to go.

It is an absolutely important framework for the organization, since its focus is on adopting positive attitudes and behaviors for collective growth.

This will increase employees' sense of belonging to the company, and encourages individual creativity for the benefit of the group.

It should be jointly established, released and posted in a conspicuous place, such as the compass points to North.

The rules, flows and organization defined in the processes, affect people's performance.

Try scratching the last letter of each of the following words:

Figure 28 - Scratching last letter, 1

Try again:

Blundering　　　　　**Awkward**　　　　　**Organized**

Figure 29 - Scratching last letter, 2

The analysis of flows that occur throughout the processes in the organization happens at the organizational level but also along the sequence of events that occurs until reaching the final product.

Depending on the company' activity, this sequence of events within the processes determines the effectiveness of the organization, and is an important element to consider in the Structure.

Regardless of the simplicity and configuration with which processes are designed, the timing of execution of different tasks is also an important aspect for the success of the organization.

You must be prepared execute the right things at the right time.

Whatever the strategy of the organization, the analysis of the processes that are used in terms of rules, flows and timings, will allow for conclusions to be drawn about the composition of the structure and the way it might enhance people and material resources.

Degrees of freedom

When we analyze the structure, we also need to consider the degrees of freedom that it offers to the organization. The structure may affect the organization flexibility's level of adopting new strategies, and / or action plans and of establishing situations with great or less third party dependence, namely, suppliers, employees and / or customers.

This is crucial to the success of the organization. Often, an organization that is overly dependent on a third-party will lose bargaining power, competitive power, and is no longer able to be a well-known reference in its industry area.

Degrees of freedom are for the structure as clothes are to the human body: if they are too tight, they will hold the movement too much!

Solidity
Established connections, supportability

The soundness of an organization depends on the connections that are established between its components: people, resources and processes.

The graphite is the substance that forms the inside of the pencil, that allows us to write but also shatters when we are scrubbing a bit, leaving the graphite to wear off on the paper.

The diamond is the hardest natural substance known to men.

Graphite and diamond are constituted by the same number of carbon atoms. They only differ in the way the atoms are bound together.

Similarly, the organization's structure has to be as solid as possible. The way the components are bound together is of overriding importance to the robustness of the organization.

The connections that are established between the carbon atoms and the graphite form a plate pack. The atoms end up being somewhat linked together, and provide two-dimensional links only, with successive layers overlapping on one another, forming graphite.

The layers forming the graphite bind weakly on each other.

With the diamond, the links that are established between the atoms are very strong. Each atom forms covalent bonds with four other carbon atoms, which allow a three-dimensional network to be formed.

The diamond structure is extremely rigid.

The glow of two distinct structures is also quite different!

Figure 30 - Graphite vs Diamond

People, resources and processes embody the Structure.

The strength of the connections between the components of the structure depends on the rational, emotional and physical connections established.

What is the proximity that exists between the components of the structure?

A good structural organization allows physical, emotional and rational sound connections to be established.

Physical and rational connections, when, for example, reliable methods for organizing and sharing workspace that are used in similar areas of work are defined, which allows rotation to be had between members of different teams within the same specialization.

A strong structural organization is based on solid emotional connections.

A strong emotional connection implies the existence of empathy, understanding and commitment among all staff.

The keywords are: communication and sharing.

The support capacity of the structure is directly related to the efforts it will be submitted to.

We often require a certain level of response from the structure, but it does not have the capacity to do so.

What do you hope to achieve by throwing four plates at once to a person who only has two hands to hold them?

The truth is that the pursuit of profit maximization has encouraged this type of gestures.

Machinery has been increasingly replacing humans in production processes. In Economics, it is often considered that production factors are divided in capital and labor. Capital, because money allows us to acquire facilities, equipment and tools. Work, because people are necessary to ensure material resources are functioning.

It is a simplification that allows us to foresee certain end results, in terms of the possible business decisions that companies can make. . It facilitates the calculation and analysis of several scenarios.

Unfortunately, it is a simplification that entails enormous welfare costs, by disregarding the talent and human genius.

"More than machinery we need humanity."

Charlie Chaplin

The responsiveness of the organization to the effort that it is submitted to, depends on the adequacy of the structure to support these efforts and depends on the frequency it is subjected to extraordinary efforts.

Communicating and sharing gestures, objectives and difficulties, increase the capacity of individual sacrifice for the collective, for the common good.

An individual's sacrifice has its limits. The greater the sacrifices involved in the performance of tasks, the less discernment in the performance and the ability to surprise positively is lower.

The organizational structure should be properly sized according to the staffs' efforts.

Quality is a multidimensional concept that is evaluated concerning different factors and perspectives that vary from person to person.

The definition of quality is seen as something that is only possible when we reduce the scope of analysis.

Cristiano Ronaldo is a quality sportsman, but only if we consider his evaluation among other footballers.

In general, having quality is to be able to surprise positively, responding to what is expected and then adding something more. Being of quality is being excellent.

Limiting ourselves to respond to what is expected without adding anything else is simply being sufficient.

The structure limits the levels of excellence that the organization can achieve and, therefore, determines its basic level of quality.

A poor structure, where the work that is produced comes out with too many defects, inaccuracies or gaps, is costly to the organization.

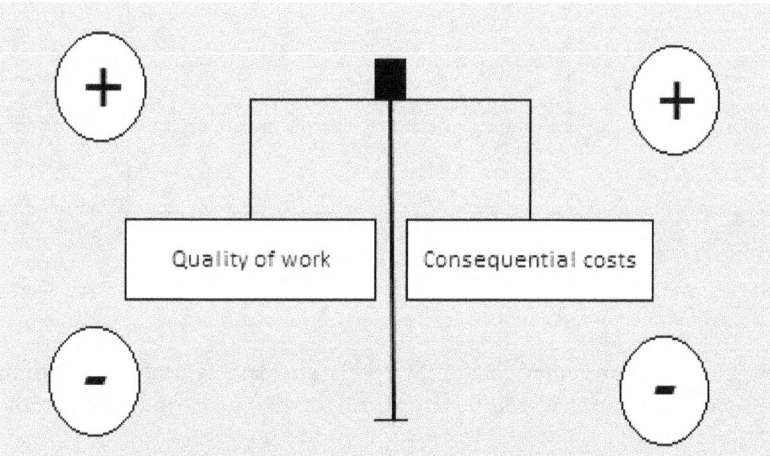

Figure 31 - Quality of work vs Consequential costs

There is equilibrium in the relationship between the quality of work that is produced and its consequential costs.

For instance, if a production line stops producing for two days due to an error within mixture of two compounds of raw materials, this lack of quality represents a cost for the company.

This cost of poor quality work rarely is quantified adequately.

The ISO 9001 is an international standard for the certification of quality management systems.

It intends to certify whether or not the organization's products and services are in line with the established rules, committing to full customer satisfaction, in a continuous improvement process.

ISO 9001 - Quality management systems
Processes aproach

Goal / Application field	Quality management system	Management responsibility	Resources management	Product realization	Measurement Analysis Improvement
Product meets customer requirements	Documentation declarations manual procedures documents documents control records control	Commit the organization	Provision of resources	Planning	Customer satisfaction
Increase customer satisfaction	Documents control	Focus on client	Human resources competency training awareness	Processes related to customer	Internal audit
	Records control	Quality policy	Infrastruture	Product requirements	Monitoring and measurement of processes
		Planning integrity planning - implementation	Work environment	Product requirements review	Monitoring and measurement of products
		Responsibility and Authority		Communication with the customer pre and post sales	Control of nonconforming product
		Internal communication		Design and Development inputs outputs review verification validation change control	Data Analysis
		Review input output		Purchases	Continuous improvement correcte actions preventive actions
				Production and service provision production control process validation identification and traceability product preservation	
				Equipment control	

Figure 32 - ISO 9001, Processes approach

The process approach that is presented in the ISO 9001 standard is useful as a guiding tool and for analysis of the construction of the several processes within the company. It shows us some of the topics on which we need to act upon.

Quality certification does not have specific data, such as the greater or lesser number of complaints recorded in a given period of time, the degree of customer satisfaction or the evolution of organizational climate.

It is intended only for certifying that the company complies with the conditions set out in the table above that, in general, rarely means that the organization has effective quality in their processes and / or in its products and services.

Companies must maintain a real demand for quality.

The structure of the organization will be crucial for:
- Quality Processing (error free process);
- Speed Processing;
- Monitoring and controlling methodologies;
- Quality of the finished product (end product well rated by customers in relation to the items considered relevant);
- Ability to surprise positively;
- Ability to achieve strategic objectives.

The structure should ensure lots of room for creativity.

2.3 EXECUTION

Execution

Execution is the Structure's way of expressing of the Strategy.
What we do must have:
- One reason (for motivation and for execution);
- One objective;
- One result.

The reason differs from objective, because it defines why we do something and the objective defines the result we want to achieve.

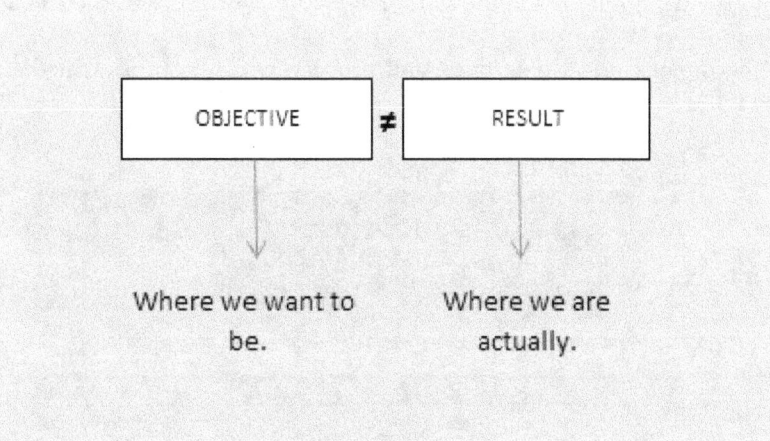

Figure 33 - Objective vs Result

Before the execution is completed, there is no guarantee that the desired objectives will be achieved.

If we have an appropriate and well-defined Strategy and Structure, it may be quite easier to obtain results that exceed the objectives, if we put actions based on motivation and monitoring mechanisms into practice.

On a daily basis or on a yearly basis, when working with the same teams, same features and in the same market, companies often ask for higher results!

More and better!

With the aid of acquired experience, continuous improvement of processes and the evolution of the strategic positioning of the company in the market, you can get it for a certain period of time, which is necessarily finite!

Doing it more times and doing it better…

Doing it better means doing it with less effort. When exhausted, we can only do the same or worse. When exhausted, we tend to lose clarity and insight.

When exhausted, the quality of work decreases.

When exhausted, the capacity to surprise positively decreases.

Doing it more times means more work is involved.

In order to do it better consistently there must be more work involved, which is done effortlessly. You must be continually inventing the wheel … You need to keep making creativity a reality!

Surprisingly, the results that give us more satisfaction to obtain are those that are achieved with great effort, after much involvement in a task, which allow us to achieve the objectives we thought were unreachable!

That is because we have surprised ourselves positively. We're classifying ourselves with an "Excellent"!

This satisfaction is something that an organization of excellence must provide to their employees, so that there is a maximum utilization of the company's potential.

This effort must exist, must be requested and must be exulted. But there must be a high dose of balance. Shortly, after such effort, the rest should be provided.

In short, to be excellent, we need to get more work done, without energy losses, and encourage the staff to make efforts in order to achieve higher competitive levels.

What is the simplest way to achieve this?

Hiring talented people.

This makes us do more things in a better way. Talent takes us further, to obtain more results with less effort. Talent makes results arise naturally.

Instead of hiring talented people, we can also discover talent internally, among members of the organization. Suit the individual skills of employees to certain functions.

Encouraging talent towards organizational objectives is achieved through monitoring and motivation processes.

Motivation processes are important for the manifestation of creativity of each individual talent, and for personal fulfillment…

Monitoring processes are crucial to keep all employees focused on collective goals.

In the first line of performance monitoring process, there are the KPIs (Key performance indicators).

As mentioned in the section "Balanced Scorecard", when setting up the organization's strategy, the definition of KPIs should cover both the organization and the staff. This is the ideal process to create a natural sense of individual contribution to the common good.

We must define the organization's objectives, and proceed while ensuring that the whole strategy is executed with these objectives in mind.

Annual KPI's - Example

Performance Indicator	Objective
Average margin of commercialization	20,00%
Return on equity	5,00%
Annual Sales	1.000.000,00

Annual Sales	1.000.000,00
Product line A	500.000,00
Product A1	200.000,00
Product A2	200.000,00
Product A3	100.000,00
Product line B	500.000,00
Product B1	170.000,00
Product B2	180.000,00
Product B3	150.000,00

Margin of commercialization	
Product A Margin	25,00%
Product B Margin	15,00%

Implementation of operational improvements	Objective
Production	6
Collections	2
Sales	6
After-Sales	6

Figure 34 - Annual KPI's example, 1

In this example, we have a set consisting of three overall financial objectives and their sub-divisions by product line.

In this example, we also have a module that aims to implement operational improvements.

Using this type of assistance tool for objective implementation, allows us to monitor the organization performance throughout the year, giving managers a greater ability to tune the sails according to the wind. Decisions are based on facts and should be ready as the information is updated.

Annual KPI's - Example

Performance Indicator	Objective	Result	Deviation	Fulfillment %
Average margin of commercialization	20,00%	22,00%	2,00%	110,00%
Return on equity	5,00%	4,00%	-1,00%	80,00%
Annual Sales	1.000.000,00	945.322,00	-54.678,00	94,53%
Annual Sales	1.000.000,00	945.322,00	-54.678,00	94,53%
Product line A	500.000,00	622.444,00	122.444,00	124,49%
Product A1	200.000,00	112.678,00	-87.322,00	56,34%
Product A2	200.000,00	245.990,00	45.990,00	123,00%
Product A3	100.000,00	263.776,00	163.776,00	263,78%
Product line B	500.000,00	322.878,00	-177.122,00	64,58%
Product B1	170.000,00	171.500,00	1.500,00	100,88%
Product B2	180.000,00	32.000,00	-148.000,00	17,78%
Product B3	150.000,00	119.378,00	-30.622,00	79,59%
Margin of commercialization				
Product A Margin	25,00%	19,00%	-6,00%	76,00%
Product B Margin	15,00%	28,00%	13,00%	186,67%

Implementation of operational improvements	Objective	Result	Deviation	Fulfillment %
Production	6	9	3	150,00%
Collections	2	1	-1	50,00%
Sales	6	4	-2	66,67%
After-Sales	6	7	1	116,67%

Figure 35 - Annual KPI's example, 2

Let us consider that, after one year, the company recorded its results on the table above.

It managed to execute what was anticipated in only one of three main items. Among its product lines and in terms of sales, it only succeeded with product "A". In terms of marketing margins, it only managed to achieve the intended target with product "B". It implemented 21 operational improvements, but the target was only reached in two out of four areas.

If an organization finishes the year with this performance, we can deduce that there were little monitoring efforts throughout the year, given the huge deviations that exist between the results obtained in different areas of the company. We can also deduce that it is an organization with communication deficits between sectors that are somewhat misaligned with each other.

One could speculate as to how some of the results were obtained. For example, we could say that, eventually, the manager of product "B" may have undertaken an action with the intent of achieving his/her individual goal of profit margin, due to his/her greed, which created a situation of greater difficulty when trying to selling the product, because of a higher selling price that was implemented by the manager.

Annual KPI's - Example

Performance Indicator	Objective	Result	Deviation	Fulfillment %
Average margin of commercialization	20,00%	22,00%	2,00%	110,00%
Return on equity	5,00%	4,00%	-1,00%	80,00%
Annual Sales	1.000.000,00	945.322,00	-54.678,00	94.53%
Annual Sales	1.000.000,00	945.322,00	-54.678,00	94.53%
Product line A	500.000,00	510.000,00	10.000,00	102,00%
Product A1	200.000,00	163.125,00	-36.875,00	81.56%
Product A2	200.000,00	245.990,00	45.990,00	123,00%
Product A3	100.000,00	100.885,00	885,00	100,89%
Product line B	500.000,00	435.322,00	-64.678,00	87,06%
Product B1	170.000,00	168.500,00	-1.500,00	99,12%
Product B2	180.000,00	144.675,00	-35.325,00	80,38%
Product B3	150.000,00	122.147,00	-27.853,00	81,43%

Margin of commercialization				
Product A Margin	25,00%	19,00%	-6,00%	76,00%
Product B Margin	15,00%	26,00%	11,00%	173,33%

Implementation of operational improvements	Objective	Result	Deviation	Fulfillment %
Production	6	6	0	100,00%
Collections	2	2	0	100,00%
Sales	6	6	0	100,00%
After-Sales	6	7	1	116,67%

Figure 36 - Annual KPI's example, 3

Let us consider again that after a year, the company would have obtained this data.

Similarly, it could only perform what was intended on only one out of three main items. Among its product lines, it only succeeded in product "A" in terms of sales. In terms of marketing margin, it only managed to achieve product "B"'s target. Also as before, 21 operational improvements were implemented, but this time the goal was reached in all operational areas.

If we conduct a more superficial analysis, the two performances seem very similar.

In which organization would you rather be?

Although they look similar, the truth is that this second company's operational execution is superior. There are considerably smaller deviations from the objectives that were set up and the actions required for operational improvement that were implemented. It is likely that, in this second company, communication is more fluid within the organization, and / or there are a greater number of monitoring actions performed throughout the year depending on the intermediate results.

In accordance with the deviations from the objectives that were observed between the two cases we have:

Case 1

Result	Global	Sales AB	Margin AB	Line A	Line B	Improvements
item 1	110,00%	124,49%	76,00%	56,34%	100,88%	150,00%
item 2	80,00%	64,58%	186,67%	123,00%	17,78%	50,00%
item 3	94,53%			263,78%	79,59%	66,67%
item 4						116,67%
Average	94,84%	94,53%	131,33%	89,67%	59,33%	95,83%
Average Deviation	10,10%	29,96%	55,33%	33,33%	41,55%	37,50%

Case 2

Result	Global	Sales AB	Margin AB	Line A	Line B	Improvements
item 1	110,00%	102,00%	76,00%	81,56%	99,12%	100,00%
item 2	80,00%	87,06%	173,33%	123,00%	80,38%	100,00%
item 3	94,53%			100,89%	81,43%	100,00%
item 4						116,67%
Average	94,84%	94,53%	124,67%	102,28%	89,75%	104,17%
Average Deviation	10,10%	7,47%	48,67%	20,72%	9,37%	6,25%

Figure 37 - Annual KPI's example, 4

From this simple case study, whose nuances apply to reality *ipsis verbis*, we can weave several important considerations:

1- The definition of objectives, by itself, does not improve the operational functioning of companies.

2- The definition of objectives and their monitoring over time, is an important aid for operational execution of business plans.

3- Concentrating excessively on objectives, transfers the focus of employees from collective interests to personal and / or internal interests, which means the focus is not on the client anymore. The client is now seen as a means to achieve objectives, rather than the final recipient of the organization's efforts.

4- In this case, the tendency to work towards statistics increases, instead of working for the common good. Focus too much on results and you will lose your view of the processes that were used to achieve them.

5- The tendency to evaluate employees based on results that were obtained increases, often without regards to the quality of their work that was in fact effectively developed, and without considering their level of knowledge, or potential.

6- If you allocate individual goals exclusively, the tendency for employees to engage in internal fighting in favor of their personal interest increases, even if this happens at the expense of the organization. You can lose the ability of staff mutually aiding each other within the organization.

7- If you allocate individual goals exclusively, the link between the individual performance and the collective goals will weaken of, which, at its limit, may lead to "functional parasitism" (despite a minor or null performance, some workers may benefit from the efforts of others).

Despite such dangers, defining mixed objectives along similar lines to those of our case study may drive the organization to transcend itself, reaching levels of performance above any prospect that initially could be conceived.

The creation of these frameworks for monitoring performance levels is crucial if you're aiming for excellence. Harmonizing the collective goals with individual goals should be a priority, allowing employees to focus everyday on doing what needs to be done.

Monitoring through KPIs is a more efficient way of doing it than monitoring with Gantt charts (you can see an example on page 26). With the GOPP methodology we limit ourselves to perform according to a previously established plan. With KPIs, we create the ambition of going beyond the planned objectives.

What takes us further: cooperation or competition?

When we interact with each other with the aim of raising our collective capacity and devoid of individual interests, we increase the number, scope and creativity of solutions that can undergo analysis.

The discussions that are held when an attitude of cooperation is present, often results in an enlargement of choices which in turn leads to the adoption of solutions that serve the interests of all best.

When we adopt a competitive attitude, we gain objectivity. We focus much more on what it takes to achieve a certain goal. We seek the solutions that are reduced to achieve a specific objective: winning!

When we reduce it this way, we lose something.

We gain objectivity, but that objectivity has a cost.

We lose diversity and creativity.

We lose the ability to surprise positively.

We lose the capacity for excellent performance.

Discussions that are overwhelmed by competitive attitudes rarely serve more than one purpose: to understand the relative strength of the parties regarding the subject under discussion.

The higher the competitive behavior, the smaller the communication established between the parties will be.

Despite the importance of monitoring processes, motivation processes are even more relevant.

Creating balance between competition and cooperation is crucial for the collective performance.

At the corporate level, there are two main sources of individual employee motivation:

1- Personal achievement

2- Material reward

For personal fulfillment to occur, people must be called to do something more than the mere task of replacing machinery. Personal fulfillment involves placing our personal stamp on the actions that are being developed. It implies the existence of room for individual creativity.

In general, employees at the beginning of their career feel okay about personal achievement because, in principle, they are in a continuous learning process and that is usually a motivating factor.

As time goes by, personal accomplishment becomes increasingly difficult to nurture.

That is why it is important that the company has room for the expression of individual creativity, while reinforcing the sense of belonging to the organization.

But personal fulfillment covers professional, family and individual fields.

Assigning material compensation (salary, cash incentives, travel and other benefits) is always important. In addition to enabling people to meet their basic needs, it can also enable personal fulfillment of ambitions outside the professional sphere.

The balance between individual and collective goals can be sought throughout the split allocation of material incentives among both, cumulatively with the defining a reward for the fulfillment of objectives in the organization.

We intend to have each employee competing with himself for the best possible outcome, and working with the organization in order to achieve extraordinary results.

Continuing with our case study, we could have set the following objectives' alignment:

Alignment Objectives	Objective	Weight %
# Areas with negative deviation = 0.00%	4	50,00%
% peer fulfillment	100,00%	50,00%

Figure 38 - Annual KPI's example, Alignment targets

Wanting to set at the end of the year a minimum number of areas with negative deviation equal to four (not six), means creating an attainable goal that is also surmountable and, at the same time, one that stimulates collective resilience. All areas and departments are now looking for each other and building bridges to spontaneous interdepartmental mutual aid.

When areas of similar performance all fulfill their objectives, this situation also promotes the cooperation between professionals that usually tend to be in direct competition with each other (a situation that could lead to one hiding a process of improvement, that could be successfully practiced in a particular department, for example).

We could also define how to calculate monetary incentives, considering the following matrix for the three fundamental objectives.

Example of monetary incentive:

Objective	Reach 100,0%	Reach 110,0%	Reach 120,0%
Individual	1,00	1,20	1,50
Collective	1,00	1,20	1,50
Alignment	1,00	1,20	1,50

Figure 39 - Annual KPI's example, Monetary incentive

Now, each employee shall be concerned with the fulfillment of objectives from other areas of the company. At the same time, they will also be concerned with the fulfillment of the objectives of those who exercise the same function.

Multiply the monetary unit for any value you want. See that it has a positive effect on the motivation of employees, while keeping them focused on the objectives that are to be achieved, individually and collectively.

Whenever someone discovers a way to improve a process, he or she has an incentive to take initiative in order to disclose said discovery to members of the organization that can take advantage of such information. This practice will foster communication and knowledge sharing.

It also fosters mutual aid.

We'll have each employee simultaneously worried about individual and collective performance, as it is desirable and rational.

Case 2

Result	Global	Sales AB	Margin AB	Line A	Line B	Improvements
item 1	110,00%	102,00%	76,00%	81,56%	99,12%	100,00%
item 2	80,00%	87,06%	173,33%	123,00%	80,38%	100,00%
item 3	94,53%			100,89%	81,43%	100,00%
item 4						116,67%
Average	94,84%	94,53%	124,67%	102,28%	89,75%	104,17%
Average Deviation	10,10%	7,47%	48,67%	20,72%	9,37%	6,25%
Average Deviation<0	-12,73%	-12,94%	-24,00%	-18,44%	-19,10%	0,00%

Figure 40 - Annual KPI's example, deviations

In our example, the calculation of the incentive for the Product Manager B would be the following:

Product Manager - Line B	Objective	Result	Deviation	Incentive
Individual objectives	Weighing	40,00%		0,30 a)
Margin of commercialization	0,15	0,26	173,33	1,50
Sales - Product line B	500000,00	435322,00	87,06	0,00
TOTAL				0,75
Collective objectives	Weighing	30,00%		0,18 b)
Average margin of commercialization	0,20	0,22	110,00	1,20
Annual Sales	1000000,00	945322,00	94,53	0,00
TOTAL				0,60
Alignment Objectives	Weighing	30,00%		0,10 c)
Implementing production improvements	6	6,00	100,00	1,00
Number of areas without negative deviation	4	1,00	0,00	0,00
% Peer fulfillment	100,00%	[1] 0,00	0,00	0,00
TOTAL				0,33
[1] Results in "0.00" because the Manager of Product A did not fulfill their individual goals.				0,58 d)

a) 0,30 = 40% x (1,50 + 0,00) / 2

b) 0,18 = 30% x (1,20 + 0,00) / 2

c) 0,10 = 30% x (1,00 + 0,00 + 0,00) / 3

d) 0,58 = 0,30 + 0,18 + 0,10

Figure 41 - Annual KPI's example, Calculation for PM - Line B

The use of three line targets has a disadvantage: greater complexity in the calculation of the annual incentives values of each employee. This increased complexity is associated with greater difficulties for people to understand its operationalization.

Once this barrier is surpassed, the organizational performance will be working and oriented towards a situation of greater capacity and resilience for achieving collective goals. This in turn will mean that the company will gain a significant competitive advantage over the competition, with very positive effects in the medium term.

Monetary incentives can be supplemented with other individual and collective compensation such as travelling, material awards, personal training, access to extraordinary events and the likes. To define this type of non-monetary compensation, it is important that the company is sure about what constitutes a motivation for employees.

Execution will not depend only on the objectivity of employees while performing their tasks.

Execution also depends on the absence of errors in the performance of tasks.

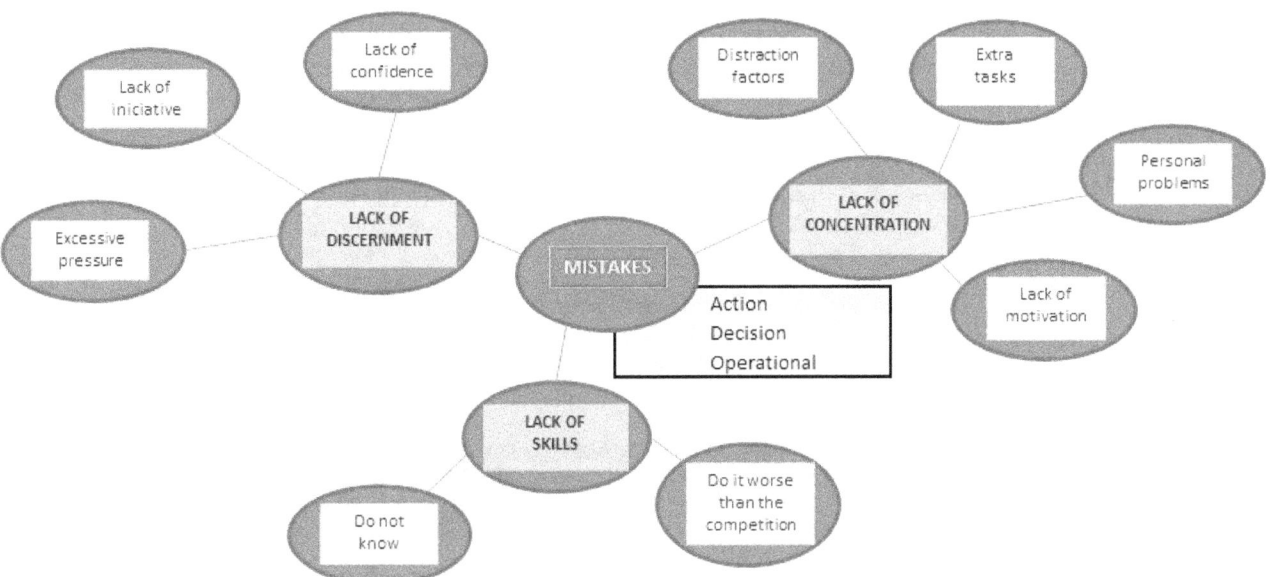

Figure 42 - Range of mistakes

There are action, decision and operational errors.

Mistakes are a direct result of three fundamental deficiencies: lack of skills, lack of insight and lack of concentration.

In turn, each of these deficiencies may be caused by clearly identifiable points. Understanding them helps the company's management to develop the correct stance and take action that minimizes or eliminates errors.

The lack of insight usually comes from emotional aspects. People do not take the right decision because they are not feeling confident, they feel pressured, or simply because they did not want to decide or defer decisions, taking a defensive attitude. There may be other causes such as excessive anxiety, but this tends to be more personal.

Lack of concentration frequently comes from functional aspects. Lack of coordination, and / or existence of poorly defined processes, can create difficulties when performing a set of tasks, thus leading to errors. Lack of concentration can also be caused by emotional issues such as personal problems, but these issues should only be a concern of the organization when they appear, simultaneously, in many collaborators.

Lack of skills for performing given tasks can be overcome with training, readjusting people, and / or hiring talented people.

However, one must be careful not to confuse the emergence of errors due to lack of concentration with lack of competence. These are different situations, and sometimes not easily distinguished from each other. It is an extremely costly mistake to fire an employee with great potential following a miscalculation of this nature.

A process of error detection and reduction will increase confidence levels of employees:
- Adequate the structure of your organization;
- Set appropriate goals;
- Demand concentration;
- Develop skills;
- Create motivating factors;
- Improve organizational communication.

Execution still depends on good operational capacity management.

Both personal fulfillment and material compensation are directly linked to motivation. The satisfaction of a job well done goes beyond material compensation.

If there is an overlapping of task functions and operations, the employee is disappointed because he feels it is more difficult to achieve the objectives that were set. And this difficulty exceeds his action radius.

Only by keeping good operational capabilities are we able to obtain the maximum positive effect resulting from the implementation of an incentive scheme similar to the one exemplified.

Keeping a good operational capacity will maintain a Positive Wave.

Optimum operational capacity will catapult the motivation of employees to higher levels, promoting individual dedication and collective pursuit of objectives. The successive achievement of individual and collective goals creates a virtuous cycle of joy and wellness within the company.

Maintaining a good operational capability is the basis of the organization and, as such, is an important responsibility for the company's leadership.

Team - Rational

	Strategy	Structure	Execution
Level 5: Continuously improve	The choices inherent to the strategy of the organization are continually put into question by the leadership of the company, trying to analyze different perspectives and possibilities. The company's culture is consolidated through effective and ongoing communication manifested in words and actions, raising service levels.	Tools, production flows and the task chain are continuously revised to increase their productivity and ensure suitability of production processes. Quality monitoring involves using internal and external resources of the organization, from different perspectives and taking full advantage of the economies of experience.	Considerations of personal fulfillment and material compensation are made to ensure efficient coordination with the definition of individual and collective objectives. The alignment of all this is a constant concern and the company ensures that the processes that increase the overall quality, either by communication, or by training.
Level 4: Focus on reliability	The leadership of the organization ensures constant vigilance regarding the internal and external circumstances over which the company evolves. The company continually prepares itself for the adversities and opportunities. Communication is fluid thus adjustments that are to be made are understood and framed within the goals to achieve.	The quality and speed of processes are based on methodologies for monitoring and control. The implementation of changes is carried out swiftly and efficiently, based on a fluid communication within the organization. The quality of the final product is enhanced by customers and there is an ability to surprise positively.	The organization ensures that the objectives that are to be achieved are in line with the operational capability of the company and are duly considered the motivational aspects of the employees. Organizational communication is working over time, over the past (partial results) and over the future (motivating effect). Higher work-intensity is possible depending on production needs.
Level 3: Make it visual	There is a widespread awareness among employees about the objectives of the organization, the model of satisfaction of customer needs and points of strength and weakness in the face of competition. The action plans are known by all and consulted whenever necessary.	It is observed that the structure presents itself adequate and adapted to the Strategy, with uniformity of processes and reduced errors and complaints. Support brackets to the proper execution of procedures are created. The communication within the company is easy and high-speed processes are in place.	Collective, individual and alignment targets are known and available to all. The monitoring engine that is available for consultation and monitoring of outcomes is regular and effective in detecting remedial needs. The occurrence of runtime errors is recorded and each type of error is properly cataloged.
Level 2: Focus on basics	The direction of the organization is aware of the intended service model and this model considers both the satisfaction of customer needs and positioning in terms of competition. The ideas and objectives are communicated to employees and there are action plans prepared.	People, facilities, equipment and tools are suitable for the pursuit of the organization's strategy. Work processes are properly defined and practices are standardized. It reinforces the connection between the entire structure, either by increasing organization and method, or through communication.	The objectives for a given period of time are previously defined . Collective, individual and alignment objectives are defined. Follow up of partial results and monitoring mechanisms are created allowing corrective actions to occur during work execution.
Level 1: Just starting	There are no specific plans for the actions taken. The ideas and goals of the organization are perceived differently from employee to employee. There is a scant consideration of the circumstances and context on which the activity is performed.	The components of the structure of the company are barely connected with each other and do not take into account the pursuit of a strategy. Work processes are not uniform and too many errors and complaints arise. The degrees of freedom given by the structure may not be proper for the organization's reality.	The results achieved at the end of a certain period of time are not compared to a framework of objectives. Actions are developed according to the individual objectives of each employee and do not always have in mind the collective goals of the organization. In general, there is no concern for the collective performance.
Place a yellow box where each area of your company is, on the Rational Levels of Achievement	**Strategy**	**Structure**	**Execution**

Figure 43 - Team, Rational

2.4 COMMUNICATION

Communication

Strategy, Structure and Execution are the rational part of any Team.

Communication is the first emotional element when building a Team.

Concerning the emotional level, there are multiple aspects that influence the interaction between employees of a company. People's culture, the company's culture, the average age of employees, hierarchical branching and / or levels of responsibility, everyone can influence the emotional behavior of the organization.

However, there are some aspects that also have an emotional impact on the organization, and its scope does not depend on the internal culture, the geographical area where the organization recruits members, or any external factor.

There are emotional factors that are present in any team, whatever their ethnic, geographical, academic, or occupational origin.

The main emotional factors that influence the performance of a team are Communication, Commitment and Mutual Aid.

For all of us, it is significantly easier to approach rational themes than to explore emotional themes.

Usually, when we explore emotional themes we end up rationalizing our thinking!

The truth is that the way we structure our emotional thinking depends on a complex set of variables. These variables depend on the circumstances, but are also dependent on the wide range of experiences that every human being has.

Every person is comparable to a mystery waiting to be discovered.

In this context, emotional flows within companies can be characterized somehow by the existence of some lack of control.

It is common to assign management up to the responsibility for the existence, or nonexistence, of good work environments.

Not being an exclusive management responsibility, there are certainly managers who determine many explicit and implicit rules which determines the team's progresses. Consequently, leadership allows, prohibits, encourages or inhibits certain behaviors between people.

For every human being, respect and dignity cannot be challenged under penalty of deterioration of the quality of relationships. For every human being, the expression of our talents raises our self-esteem.

Often, companies deliberately ignore the emotional aspect of the organization. They assume that the employee must always be "professional", keeping an "exemplar" posture, regardless of personal problems that can afflict him.

In this type of organizations, people tend to maintain a cold posture and distance themselves. They lose "proximity". They lose capacity for empathy, understanding and commitment. They are only keeping relationships for mutual interest.

The involvement of people in a certain activity may be forced or voluntary.

When such involvement is forced, the lack of will to do something does not lead to good results.

Only the voluntary involvement can catapult the results of a company.

Human beings have a tendency to lean back, to act within their comfort zones, and to avoid taking risks or making efforts that they consider unnecessary.

This facet puts a barrier facing off results that can be achieved.

This barrier must be removed.

It is welcome that participation is mandatory through all organization, with a strong focus on achieving results, so that the participant may concentrate his/her full energies on the task ahead rather than what he would do normally.

This mandatory participation should be accompanied with certain statements, such as the reasons why actions are currently being done and noting the significance and purpose of the company. This way, one reaches the sense of voluntary participation, and positions the team in such a way that it is ready to work towards achieving excellent performance.

Excellent performance, for a team, is only possible when the participants contribute actively with creative action proposals.

This participation of organization members increases the capacity of the group beyond levels that management could have considered as possible.

And so this is a way of accomplishing the "impossible"…

In mostly rational companies, there are serious communication deficits, and performances are rarely excellent.

Communication is possible when dissenting opinions are encouraged and trust is earned.

Respect, open-mindedness, unity and cooperation, participation and commitment are important values here. You may work with different people, while sharing common goals!

In companies that are mostly rational, instead of communication, there is information!

Be aware of the difference between information and communication:

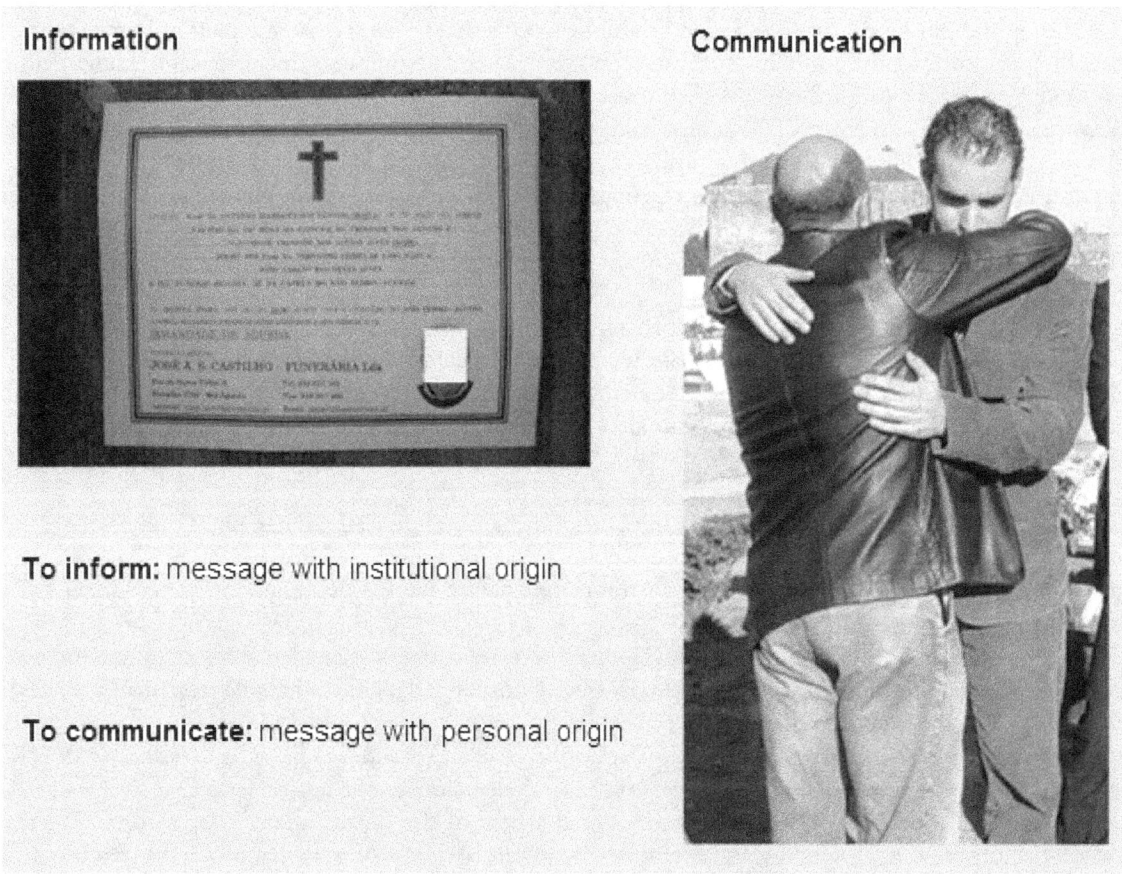

Figure 44 - Information vs Communication

Informing is essentially a one-way process.

Communicating is a two way process.

When the company manages its interpersonal relationships based on information processes, people tend to look, hear and talk.

But looking does not always means to see; hearing does not always means to understand and speaking does not always means to say.

Communicating implies noting, listening and expressing.

Communicating implies being authentic and genuine.

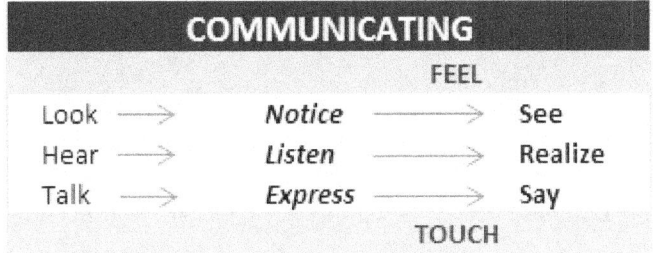

Figure 45 - Communicating: Feel - Touch

For communication to be fluid within the organization, it needs to happen spontaneously. There must be a natural concern for other colleagues, and an overall willingness to help and to be helped.

Communication involves sharing!

Communication is a voluntary act that is established in good faith.

When communication is established it is expected that it returns back.

Communicating is important for an excellent performance to be achieved by any Team.

In an organization, managers assume an important role: to create a sense of unity.

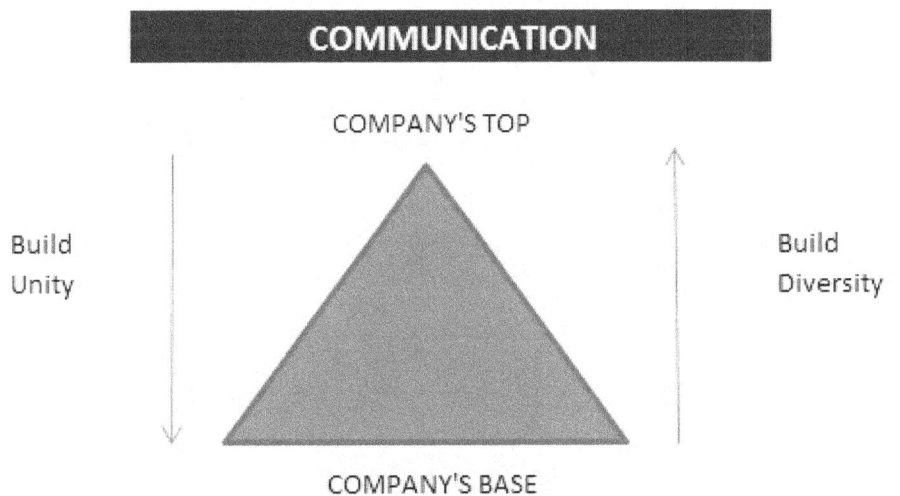

Figure 46 - Build, unity and diversity

Supervisors also assume an important responsibility: creating diversity. To do this, they need to exhibit a high capacity for listening, especially in front of their subordinates.

We all have that creative ability.

For this creative ability to be manifested, people must feel that they are not under a threat (of losing their jobs, of ridicule, of being offended, etc.). Only then one creates an environment conducive to innovation, creative abilities and / or their talents, in its entire splendor. People still need to want to do it. They must feel that their ideas can be accepted, and that they have freedom of expression to express those thoughts.

Good faith, respect and dignity are the keywords in order for an organization to be committed to excellence when communicating.

Only through communication one can release creativity and maintain the ability to surprise positively.

You have to communicate to be excellent!

"Creativity is based on the fusion of intuition and reason."

Jonas Salk

The explosion of creativity arises when the basis of the organization communicates to the top what they feel about the current situation, presenting different proposals, different aspects, and multiple perspectives and approaches.

The establishment of a two-way communication enriches and strengthens the company.

Effective communication is extremely difficult to achieve.

What we think rarely translates into what we are able to say. Here, there is a loss between what we feel and what we can communicate.

In most communication channels that we use, "noise" often arises preventing the message from being fully understood.

Finally, the recipient receives the message "his own way". We say "His own way", because the interpretation that each of us have from what we see and hear depends on our own individual references, resulting from experience accumulation and concepts acquired over time, and differing from person to person.

The ability of an individual to express him/herself, and the ability of the receiver to listen, dictates the effectiveness of communication. The differences between them, in terms of personal references and symbols, cause the interpretation of the message to vary between actors across the communication process.

What is thought by the one who is sending the message is almost always different from what is perceived by the receiver.

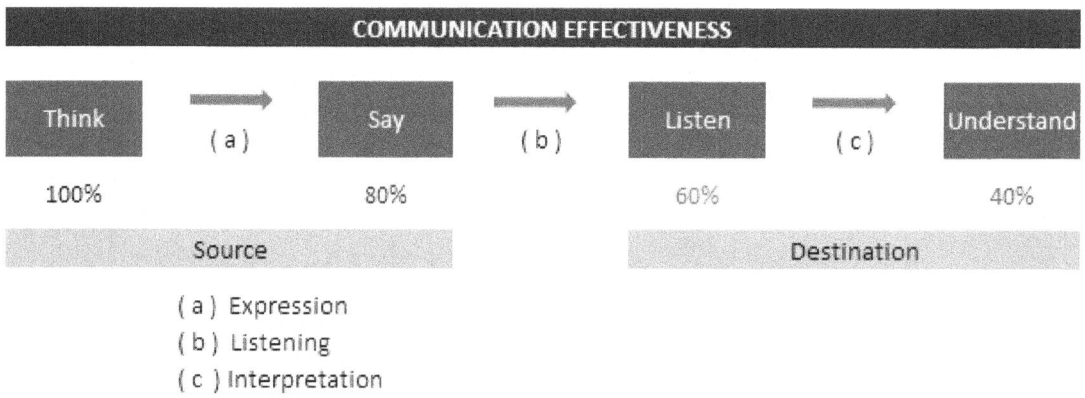

Figure 47 - Communication effectiveness

In order for communication to exist, the sender and the receiver have to switch positions, often and intermittently.

In an organization, the managers have to expose their principles and views and be able to listen to employees accordingly, by asking questions such as:

- What are your suggestions?
- What is your opinion?
- What is the reason for you to be considering this solution?

A good communicator has a greater ability to express their ideas and opinions; a lot of humility can be learned from other people: listen carefully and understand.

What is the biggest enemy of communication?

Prejudice.

Prejudices are enemies of communication. Beware of the concepts you have internalized. Although they may have had applicability in the past, the future will often present you with a different reality.

Does our concept still apply?

The decisions we take daily and the actions we make are based on the assumption that they are the best option we have, given the information available. Parts of this "available information" are prejudices that we have. They are what we think it is true. Given the present circumstances, what we believe to be true determines the way we communicate. Often, we are so certain of being right, that we give up our ability to observe before taking a decision. We fail to collect additional information.

We talked to our son without realizing he is listening to music with his headphones placed on…

Improved communication in an organization needs to pass through the development of a proper sharing culture that encourages dialogue.

This development has to be based on a structured set of practices, so that communication happens spontaneously, voluntarily, routinely and mandatorily!

It may seem a contradiction to state that the communication should be voluntary and mandatory. Let me explain. Voluntary, because it has to arise from people's will. Mandatory, because it has to happen! We need to have a sense of obligation, to demand ourselves and others a certain set of behaviors, attitudes and outcomes. Otherwise, there can be no excellence. We just have to ensure that this is processed properly, and in a healthy way.

When developing communication we need to consider its formal aspects:
- Environment, where the process is developing;
- The means of communication;
- The channel;
- The form of the message.

Depending on organization's culture and their own internal specificities, we must seek to find the most appropriate ways to foster communication within the company. A certain format, the means of communication and the propagation channel can be suitable for a certain company at a given time, and not suitable for another.

The company's leadership should understand the kind of freedom of communication that exists in the organization: freedom of expression, freedom of choice, freedom of action.

After understanding the degrees of freedom, we must question: at what hierarchical levels are some skills expressed? Which skills?
- Listening skills;
- Ability for conducting a constructive debate;
- Ability to find joint solutions.

There is no proximity without mutual trust. There is no emotional closeness without empathy, understanding or commitment.

To foster mutual trust is to make the company a good place to be.

This is achieved by improving the process of communication.

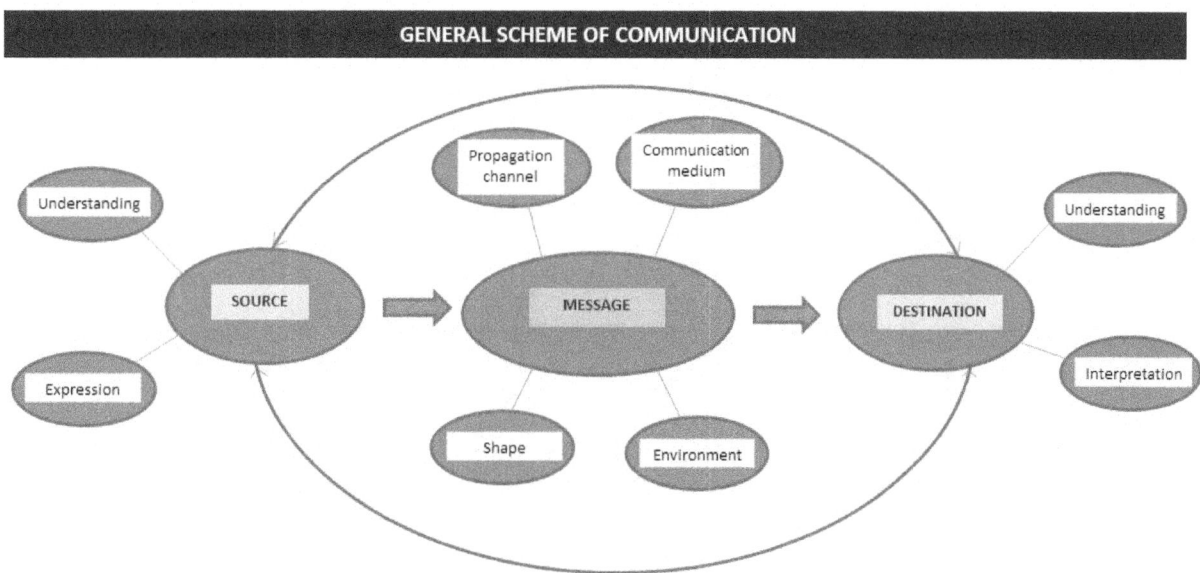

Figure 48 - Communication, general scheme

How can we foster communication within the company?

Ahead, we will see how maintaining a mechanism of Structured Information Support and a process of Focused Simplification, contributes decisively for elevating communication within the company.

2.5 COMMITMENT

Commitment

How to get full commitment from the entire organization?

This is not an easy question to answer.

This kind of task gets a little easier if we start by identifying the reasons why people do not endeavor their best efforts.

Some of the reasons are as follows:

- Self-indulgence;
- Indifference;
- Demotivation.

Self-indulgence

For each of us, it is very comfortable and desirable to get what we need without effort on our part.

This is a major reason for lack of commitment to happen. It is inherent to human nature the adherence to the "law of the least necessary effort ".

In the past, managers understood this condition in their subordinates, and invented the whip!

A laziness attitude, as it is not acceptable, it must be understood and fought.

Lack of commitment attitudes often arise because people feel lack of confidence. A person tries to do as little as possible to avoid exposing him/herself to others' criticism.

We have a 2 for 1 discount situation: it naturally becomes convenient not having to strain oneself and this kind of attitude is still "rewarded" with criticism protection…

When self-indulgence arises as a consequence of a situation of lack of confidence on the part of the employee, it is necessary to provide him or her with an adequate environment that may help highlight his/her potential, and increase his/her security when performing tasks.

In these cases, one must be aware that the transition from a stage of indulgence to a dedication stage requires the traversal of a path whose length is relatively long.

In other cases, when the employee considers that ensuring his/her salary is sufficient without caring about anything else, you need to help create in him his own discipline, developing a culture of progress and personal growth.

Indifference

Indifference is the enemy of commitment. Being less frequent than self-indulgence or lack of motivation, indifference is extremely difficult to fight.

Indifference means a deep devaluation of work. It distinguishes itself from self-indulgence, though both happen consciously. While with self-indulgence the worker seeks to do the least amount of things possible, when indifferent the worker devalues his own work and the group's work, by assigning the same value to what is being done regardless of the effort or the end result that was produced.

Change the behavior of these people implies perceiving what is valued by them. It implies understanding which functions and tasks will they attach any real meaning to.

Demotivation

Demotivation is the main cause of lack of commitment.

Demotivation is distinguished from indifference because an unmotivated person still values his work.

An unmotivated individual is not currently obtaining satisfaction with his work.

Demotivation may have a wide range of causes, but, there are some that origin in the organization itself:

- Supervisors and / or colleagues who criticize and / or ridicule other employees unjustifiably;
- Setting objectives perceived as unattainable;
- Performing tasks successively "sabotaged" by external factors to the individual (e.g. when intermittent failures of electrical current prevent a factory from working properly, several times over a month);
- Feeling that the effort is not sufficiently rewarded;
- Allocation of misfit tasks, which make the employee feel that he or she is forced to do something he does not like (e.g. assigning to the Director of Human Resources the responsibility to choose to lay off six employees by the simple pretense of reducing costs);
- Feeling he/she has to do something he/she does not agree with (like being asked to sell toothpaste to edentulous).

Demotivation is different from self-indulgence, also because an unmotivated individual can even work hard, but does it without joy, and with a performance that is below his own potential.

For an employee to be committed, we have to fight self-indulgence, indifference and lack of motivation, and promote joy.

In a workgroup, we have to get everyone's commitment and satisfy individual needs.

In the chapter "Getting Started", we saw that people's behaviors are conditioned by a cultural framework (what we believe, habits, practices and traditions), and a picture of individual motivations (money, power, recognition, fulfillment, security, pleasure, independence / autonomy and other necessities).

To motivate people to take action, it is necessary to build secure foundations: clearly defining what you want to achieve, and create a sound environment of trust and discipline.

Create in employees a sense of cultural identity, giving meaning and purpose to their individual actions and activities of the company, in a union of shared values.

We recognize the commitment when we found that the person gave his or her best with dedication, determination and intensity.

Intensity must have a temporal perpetuity. It involves having the patience to achieve the desired result, and the persistence to overcome the difficulties that arise, with unwavering faith.

When there is commitment, there is focus and objectivity.

In an organization, so that there are committed employees, they have to feel they are a part of something great. They should recognize and be recognized, paving their way together, step by step. Longer distances are achieved after overcoming the closest obstacles. Remember the defeat as the errors that occurred when we tried to score. Victories are celebrated properly.

Commitment is not due to chance.

A team's commitment is the result of a well-designed and well communicated rational sphere (in terms of strategy and structure) which allows people's behaviors to evolve naturally towards meeting their individual needs.

Maintaining the levels of commitment in employees is a direct result of the company's ability to meet individual motivations (picture), respecting the cultural frame that each person has.

In short, we can say that the organization needs to create conditions for personal development, allowing employees to exercise the tasks to which they attribute true meaning. This way, you can pursue individual and collective goals, making each worker to feel that this organization is his/her place.

A committed organization has a well-defined culture.

You must always be alert to prevent situations that can trigger demotivation, indifference and self-indulgence. The higher the levels of communication within the company, the greater the possibility of these situations to be reported in early stages, and the disciplinary capacity of the organization will be enhanced. People do what they need to do, because they want to do it. People put intensity in their actions, because they want to achieve their objectives.

People will be committed, because they will feel confident in the actions that they develop, and are satisfied with the results they get.

Being committed means being properly rewarded, whether at the material or at the emotional level.

A committed organization has, naturally, a significant competitive advantage.

2.6 MUTUAL AID

Mutual aid

To help and to be helped.

Mutual aid arises naturally when there are common collective goals for two or more people.

However, identification of common collective goals is not enough for mutual aid to occur between people. There must be a minimum condition of trust between the parties, and a sincere desire to contribute positively for others' well-being.

Confidence comes from a successive number of positive responses that each element gives to others, meeting their expectations.

Trust has an immense value that should be underlined.

Consequently, actions that may lead to the breakdown of trust between members of the organization must be completely eliminated or reduced as much as possible.

When we trust each other, we transform into a helpful resource.

When we trust each other, we have more resources within the company.

People will focus on what their peers are doing well, ask for help, and learn from them.

Quality is preferable to quantity. It is preferable that each employee remains active, attentive and available and, in addition, visible, responsible and competent.

From interaction between people, a natural sense of gratitude ultimately emerges.

This is a kind of healthy gratitude that does not need immediate feedback.

Confidence and honesty remains, and each person is authentic when performing certain actions, genuine when having certain reactions and professionally competent. Mutual respect eventually consolidates.

The first keyword for mutual aid is trust.

In an organization where people rely on each other's capabilities, have well identified collective goals, and are endowed with the ability to communicate effectively, mutual aid will be a reality. If there is willingness to help, they will feel free to ask for help.

I believe this design can be severely disrupted by conflicts of interest driven by individual unbridled ambitions.

Often, those who want power devalue the work of their peers, highlight the little they do before their supervisors, and hide information that could facilitate the work of other colleagues.

By behaving this way, they will undermine the confidence of the group.

Confidence is shaken, along with the relationship of this individual with other colleagues, and the remaining staff. This, in turn, makes them adopt a defensive and/or counteroffensive posture. Mutual aid becomes a mirage.

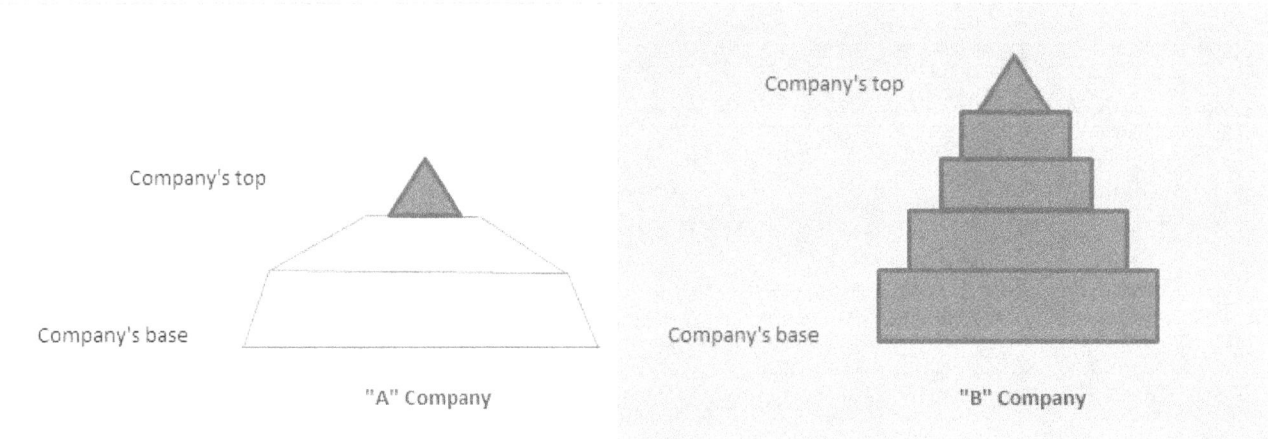

Figure 49 - Company's top vs Company's base

In which company would you rather be?

Negative and individualistic attitudes will be more frequent in company "A", or in company "B"?

Companies which are characterized by intermediate hierarchies there is a natural trend for workers to prioritize their vision of individual goals and progression in the company. This effect is smaller in companies where the hierarchy is more "flattened".

People in the company "B" are far from the top of the company. They have a greater need to make themselves look noticeable. The top seems so inaccessible that is wiser starting doing what has got to be done right now, in order to get there... And not always the most adequate means are used.

When internal competition is increasing, this makes people more individualistic when performing their daily actions.

In Company "A", people are closer and feel more "equality". Naturally, people treat each other with a different type of open-mindedness. Mutual aid comes much more frequently, and the whole organization takes advantage of this.

The struggle for power and for the promotion will not be as fierce.

Given the identical potential of each human resource, company "A" acquires a significant competitive advantage by becoming more efficient and, ultimately, with much greater capacity for innovation.

In the organization, mutual aid significantly depends on the following factors:

- Employee confidence in their abilities and those of his/her colleagues;
- Identification of collective goals;
- Effectiveness of organizational communication;
- Complexity of the hierarchical structures that are defined.

In a company where people are exercising their duties, when an individual effort is complemented by collective mutual aid, the organization will inevitably be on track to success.

	Team - Emotional		
Level 5: Continuously improve	The company fosters a culture of dialogue and sharing. Abhors up prejudices and provides incentives to conduct good faith, respect and dignity. This is a commitment by the organization for excellence in communication.	The company stimulates the level of communication so that the situations of lack of commitment are dealt with early, looking to restore confidence and intensity. It is continuously creating opportunities for personal development of employees, looking for tasks to be full of meaning for the performer.	The way communication flows between hierarchical and departmental structures is continuously evaluated to ensure mutual assistance and sharing of common objectives. Competence in performance of tasks is continually assured and disseminated in order to promote cooperation in the pursuit of individual and collective objectives.
Level 4: Focus on reliability	The channel and the form of the messages are taken care of in order to facilitate interpretation and understanding. It encourages mutual trust in professional relationships. It guarantees participation in the processes of communication within the company.	The mechanisms of individual and collective rewards are revised whenever they reveal loss of efficacy. The allocation of tasks is set, and external factors such as "sabotage" are eliminated.	People focus on what their peers are doing well and learn from them. Communication is facilitated and encouraged. Any action that might lead to the breakdown of trust between members of the organization is subject to immediate disciplinary action.
Level 3: Make it visual	Freedom of speech is encouraged throughout the company so that the creativity of everyone may be harnessed for the common interest. Actions of individual initiative in favor of the collective are developed, and disseminating information and sharing knowledge are common in the company.	High level intensity and joy at work are observed. There often occurs manifestations of positive surprise by customers when facing the service's end results. The company's strategy is well communicated and the structure feels adequate. There is an overall satisfaction with the results.	The manifestation of trust between employees is visible, with frequent interaction while performing tasks. There are well identified collective goals properly articulated with individual objectives. Each employee remains active, attentive and available within the company. There is obvious proximity and fairness in relationships.
Level 2: Focus on basics	Important information is disseminated through various means and can be consulted under initiative. The company promotes closeness and fosters mutual confidence through constructive discussions on topics of interest to the company. Relationships often occur by mutual interest.	The purpose and meaning of company's actions are understood and accepted by employees. The pursuit of individual and collective goals are based on appropriate mechanisms for material and personal rewards. The emotional rewards are considered and assigned.	The company defines common objectives among employees and creates conditions in order to establish effective communication between the parties. The complexity of the hierarchical structure is as simple as possible, fostering closeness and equity in relationships.
Level 1: Just starting	Employees are informed of what is considered to be important via hierarchical structure without major concerns in explaining why things are done a certain way. Supervisors define what should be done, when and how. Employee feedback from the base of the company is not taken into consideration. Relationships occur primarily by self-interest.	Behaviors of complacency, indifference and lack of motivation can be observed in the organization. Objectives are perceived as unattainable. Focus and objectivity are not always present when performing tasks. The customer is rarely positively surprised by the company.	Employees play a dominant behavior in pursuit of their personal goals, without attaching importance to the performance of their colleagues. The need to resort to a colleague in the performance of a task is something unpleasant and sometimes avoided.
Place a yellow box where each area of your company is, on the Emotional Levels of Achievement	**Communication**	**Commitment**	**Mutual Aid**

Figure 50 - Team, Emotional

The importance of company's culture

There are multiple studies focusing on the importance of employee motivation for the success of your business.

At a time when it is seen that the machine is replacing man in many tasks relatively easily, the difficulty of controlling emotional aspects is one of the biggest challenges faced by organization leaders today.

The same technology is often within the reach of your company and all of your competition.

The same is not true about the capacity for emotional control (of the organization).

Regardless of whether communication abilities of organization leaders are better or worse, companies that implement simple mechanisms that foster healthy interaction among its members will significantly improve communication.

The emotional power of the staff in its entirety is based on these three fundamental aspects: Communication, Commitment and Mutual Aid.

When the rational and the emotional powers are fully developed within the organization, the dynamics of a successful team are permanent.

Therefore, the company is a good place to be.

The company's culture is the unifying glue that binds the Rational and Emotional powers of a Team.

Understanding the company's culture requires us to understand the emotions in the company.

António Damásio, in his book "The Feeling of What Happens" demonstrates that an unconscious emotion produces results that translate into actions and behaviors. It also demonstrates that the actions that were produced are proportional to the emotional value of rewards that were received.

Several scientists have shown that the preferences of the human being can be learned unconsciously and very quickly.

António Damásio explains how consciousness and emotion cannot be separated in the mind of a human being.

Emotions are followed by feelings. The feeling is when the body becomes aware of its emotions. Positive emotions dictate consistent positive feelings, which in turn dictate consistent positive actions grounded in a general sense of well-being.

And the reverse can also be true, if the company is full of negative emotions.

Emotions are underlying behaviors. According to Damásio, culture is expressed in the way the human being behaves during an emotion and after an emotion.

Given the emotion, the organism can evolve in different ways.

When it triggers an emotion, we have an action resulting from an automatic behavior that may or not be perceived by us (as it happens when, for example, we are scared and immediately adopt a defensive position, an escape movement or a counterattack maneuver).

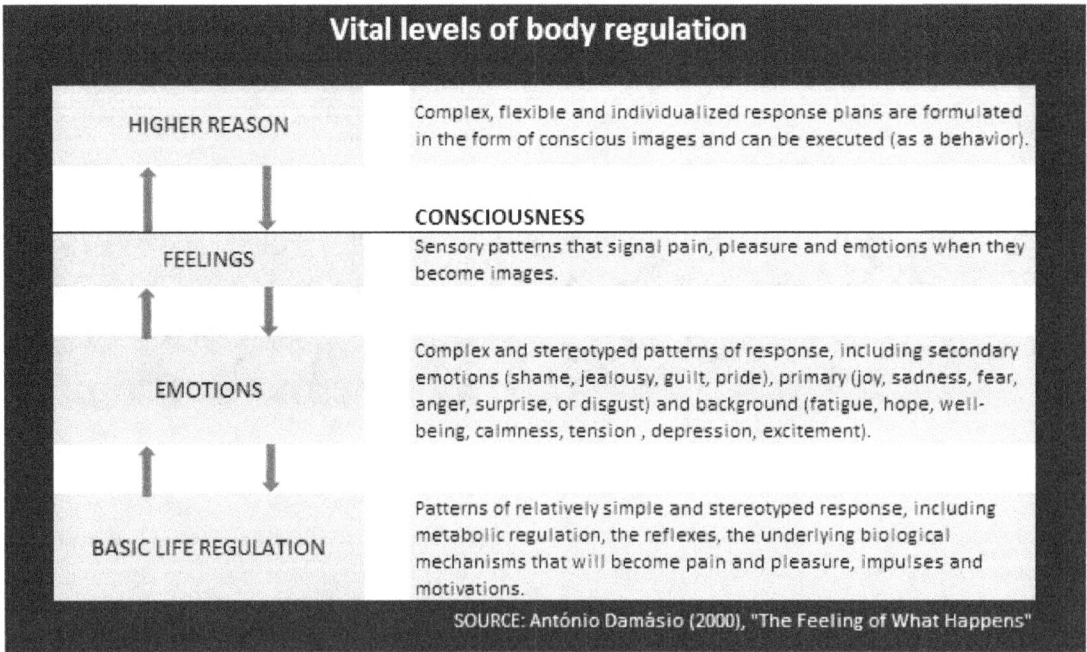

Figure 51 - Vital levels of body regulation

"A well-directed emotion seems to be the support system without which the edifice of reason cannot function effectively."

António Damásio

A correct, and well communicated strategy, explains the organization's purpose and the meaning of their existence. Inherently, each employee realizes the reason for the organization's existence, and what is the scope of the good performance of their duties. There is a set of emotional values embraced by the company with which the employee identifies himself.

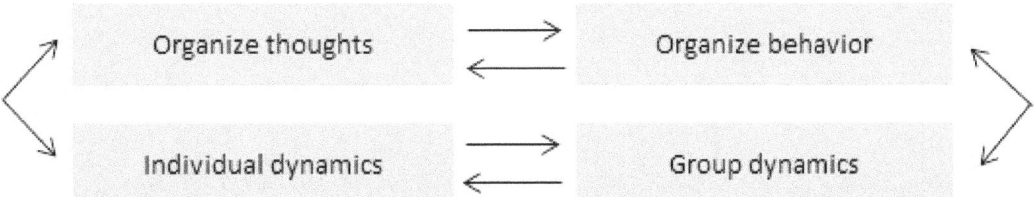

Figure 52 - Toughts and dynamics

This message needs to be reinforced and communicated within the company. It could be signaled and symbolized.

If a particular concept is part of the company's culture, then the words and deeds of all should correspond to that concept perfectly.

There is a conduct code, whether explicit or implicit.

Culture will give consistency to the team, providing the perfect link between strategy, structure and execution, and behavioral deviations that may compromise the values of the company are not allowed.

Is there any interpersonal and interdepartmental consistency in your company?

What non-material values reflect the way you think, act and feel about your organization?

2.7 STRUCTURED INFORMATION SUPPORT

Structured Information Support

The Structured Information Support mechanism is a liaison between the rational and emotional parts of the organization.

If we build a real team which is competent when defining the strategy, we will have a strong and proper structure and a staff who is determined to perform the tasks that will lead to getting over objectives, with effective communication and a strong collective; where commitment and mutual aid are present. In addition, we need to ensure that the team holds itself together in a consistent way, over time.

The soundness of the organization cannot depend on their leaders alone, cannot depend on a specific employee and cannot depend on any external factor. If it does so, it will perish!

Maintaining the strength of the organization depends on the effective mechanisms that the same organization was able to create, which, in turn, encourage desirable behaviors among all, in the present and in the future.

> **Comunicare**
>
> Latin: Becoming common.

This support allows communication to be established based on a common professional language, that is understood by all.

In few words, it is a facilitator of personal and interdepartmental interactions.

It is always regrettable when colleagues disagree about the "proper" procedure to be adopted in the same situation.

We have the perception that something is not right in an organization when we pose a question and receive two different responses from employees of the same company.

Do you agree?

In these cases, we can assume that one of them is competent, as if it was true.

The reality is that, most of the time, these situations occur because it is a symptom of the absence of an structured information support mechanism to enable communication, consultation and expeditiously learning of internal processes within the organization.

Those involved may even be wrong about what the leadership of the organization wants to happen!

There will be failures in communication.

Besides being a symptom of a lack of an organization's efficacy at the eyes of the customer, these conditions may also contribute to the degradation of the work environment and individual demotivation.

Under any prism of analysis, we conclude that these are situations should not happen when we want to maximize human and material resources that we have available.

Scientists did an experiment with five monkeys.

They placed five monkeys in a cage.

In the center of the cage a relatively high ladder was placed, on top of which, randomly and intermittently, there was from time to time an appealing bunch of bananas.

Whenever a monkey climbed the stairs to eat the appetizing bananas, the other four monkeys that were on the ground were wet with water through hoses directed by scientists.

The four monkeys that stayed on the soil were soaked everytime a monkey climbed the stairs to the top to feast on bananas.

After a few occurrences, when the bananas emerged at the top of the stairs and a monkey began to climb the ladder, the others sought to prevent him from climbing, grabbing him and assaulting him.

After a few sessions of beatings, scientists continued to put bananas there but failed to wet the soil monkeys since none tried to reach the bananas on top of the ladder.

As a result of this behavior of the group, after a few more appearances of bananas, the monkeys left entirely to try to reach the bananas.

At this time, scientists replaced an old monkey in the cage for another completely new.

When the appetizing bunch of bananas first came to the new monkey in the cage, he tried to climb the ladder immediately and also immediately, four others grabbed him and beat him so that he did not.

Since no monkey reached bananas scientists didn't wet any monkey.

After a short time, to prevent the attacks, the new monkey was no longer trying to reach the bananas when they appeared at the top of the stairs.

The scientists then replaced one of the four veteran monkeys and introduced a new monkey in the cage.

This new monkey returned to go through the same process as last one: he tried to reach the bananas, was beaten and left to trying, without ever having been wet.

The replacement of veteran monkeys that were from the beginning continued until in the cage resided five monkeys that had never been wet before.

Although bananas did appear as appetizing as ever, they continued to prevent each other from reaching the bunch of bananas on ladder's top, grabbing and assaulting.

If we ask them why were they preventing the other monkeys to climb the ladder, the initial five monkeys might reply that did not want to be wet, but the final five monkeys could only reply that whenever it happened they respond with that behavior, but wouldn't know how to explain why.

Figure 53 – The experience with monkeys

The construction of the "SIS - Structured Information Support", will allow each employee to focus exactly on the role he or she deserves within the organization, during the exercise of his/her functions.

For the success of any company, we need to define the right things, how can we do the right things, and how can we accomplish the right things in the right way.

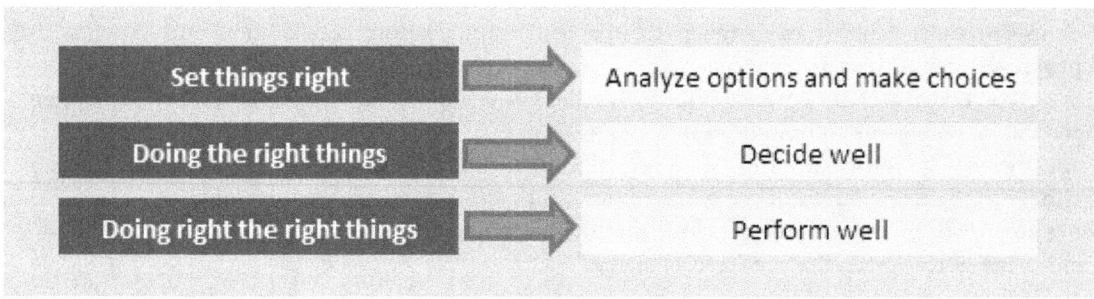

Figure 54 - Right things

The SIS will allow people whose functions mostly concern execution, to focus almost exclusively on execution.

Similarly, people whose functions are mostly concerned on analysis and coordination can also focus their attention on the correct choice of actions to take.

This greater focus on the job requirements will encourage improvement suggestions from workers, which are mostly centered around process simplification and, usually, with creative solutions.

If the organization lets each employee perform the tasks "your way", each person must find his/her own solution to every problem. This option will imply a greater amount of difficulties for the managers of the company: coordinating efforts and find effective solutions to joint problem solving.

Usually, organizations have one or more support mechanisms, so that the information that has to be used by employees is available.

The structure of that information, its availability and the way it presented to employees, is what determines the effectiveness of its use.

The existence of a structured support for information brings a number of advantages to the company:

1- Adaptability of training needs
   a. The employee can be autodidact; proactive in the pursuit of knowledge and his/her individual valuation;
   b. Information shall always be available in a time of need;
   c. People will feel competent.

2- Cost reduction
   a. It immediately reduces workers' training needs;
   b. It fosters the reduction of operational errors;
   c. It promotes the reduction of conflicts in the workplace and trust between employees.

3- Productivity increase
   a. Contribution towards a fluid and articulate operability;
   b. Labor interactions become more objective, balanced and less dependent on individual subjectivity;
   c. People will feel confident while executing their tasks.

4- Communication
   a. Expressing what was meant to be said will be closer to the interpretation of what was actually said, thus facilitating an understanding between the sender and the receiver of a message;
   b. Communication becomes more fluid and effective within the organization;
   c. Communication between people shall be made primarily to consolidate knowledge rather than a merely intermittent transmission of basic knowledge;
   d. People will feel confident (in themselves and in the organization).

Organizations that show greater efficiency when using available information, have an important source of differentiation in their ability to surprise positively, and have a competitive advantage over competitors given their increase in productivity and reduction of operating costs.

Typically, the value of a theory depends on its practical use.

The real challenge is the transition from theory to practice…

With the creation of a Structured Information Support, we aim to ensure the fulfillment of two fundamental principles:
1- Unity and Convergence
2- Security and Confidence

Unity and Convergence

It is important that the organization speaks with one voice only, and is able to reason over a main line of thought.

Because each individual provides his/her contribution in various forms, there is a need to converge individual efforts into the pursuit of collective goals.

The construction of the Structured Information Support should be based on the principle of Unity and Convergence.

Security and Confidence

The operational execution of tasks depends on the levels of effectiveness and efficiency, shown by employees in the exercise of their functions. The greater the confidence with which the articulated operations are done, the greater the capacity of the organization to recognize organizational capacity in itself, and the greater the confidence that is established among its members, by various interactions.

The security I am talking about, is the security we feel when we know we are proceeding correctly, as recommended by the organization, without the risk of error and / or being criticized.

It is the security we feel when we know that we did well, regardless of the potential exposure to any kind of criticism.

This is the kind of security that raises the confidence level of any performer, in any activity.

Based on these two principles, we move forward to define the method to use when building the Structured Information Support.

Usually, there is a wide range of instructions, scattered manuals, internal emails, instructions, announcements and verbal instructions that are never placed on physical media. In many organizations, day-to-day practices are rooted in the past, without questioning or explaining why things are done.

In a multi-departmental organization, people hold different perspectives among themselves, depending on the nature of their duties and in accordance with their own individuality.

The solution to the same problem usually differs from person to person.

Within the same company, it is desirable that the solution to a given problem is unique, in accordance with the principle of "Unity and Convergence".

Consequently, it is necessary to make a survey of all practices developed within the organization, and proceed towards standardizing the solution to the same problem, in harmony with the principles of "Unity and Convergence" and "Security and Trust".

I propose that the method is based on four steps:

1- **Identifying needs**
2- **Understanding actions**
3- **Standardizing practices**
4- **Managing the unexpected**

Step 1, "Identifying needs," aims to identify all actions that are taken in the company and identifying dependency networks within the organization.

Step 2, "Understanding the actions", aims to identify why are certain actions being carried out and their consequences, noting opportunities to reduce costs, for productivity gains, identifying sources of conflict and sources of error.

Step 3, "Standardizing practices", aims to identify appropriate practices, and proceed to record them on a digital support.

Step 4, "Managing the unexpected", aims to find those responsible for certain actions and finding concrete procedures for managing what is unforeseen.

Construction of SIS - Structured Information Support

Although it can seem like a megalomaniac task, the fact is that each task is as big as complexity of the structure of the company makes it to be.

Tasks can be implemented in two ways: either it calls for the involvement of all, or a small team can be created and, this way, dedicated to collecting, analyzing and compiling the information above.

The first option will allow one to obtain a broad range of practices, which will be gathered from several in various individual's perspectives. This will enrich the available information and alert us to situations where those responsible were not minimally aware of the situation. You should choose this option if all employees participate actively and enthusiastically.

Involving all employees in this process is also involves promoting greater receptivity to the use of the Structured Information Support mechanism, along with the development and consolidation of a sense of belonging to the organization and raising the overall knowledge of this tool and of the company itself that each employee has.

The creation of a small team that can survey all actions taken by the organization, in addition to identifying the reason of their practices, and the existence of functional dependence networks between people and departments can be effective when you want speed and greater objectivity when building the Structured Information Support. However, you will lose some of the individual or departmental perspectives on issues that may be important, in order to find the best solutions for the organization.

Eventually, this deficit can be exceeded through the use of the Focused Simplification process that we will see further ahead, and this gain in speed can be important for the company.

The basis of the Structured Information Support mechanism are the actions performed by employees.

In this context, it is important to understand a little about the action itself, in a more theoretical context, and afterwards we can produce a practical tool for obtaining relevant information for the company.

Any action can be characterized as having an origin, a scope, a purpose, a form and a result. Additionally, we weave relevant considerations regarding the frequency with which an action takes place, the inherent dependent relationships in an organization, and the possibility of outbreaks of conflict associated with the action.

The origin is the "trigger" of the action. For example: If a customer asks the barman "A Gin Tonic, please!", here, the customer order is the origin of the action, which is the drinks' preparation.

At the origin of the action, we can have our own initiative, an instruction or a suggestion from others.

Facing the action's "trigger", an active collaborator will have a certain response: delegate, execute, ignore or postpone the task.

The action is developed within a given context. In the example above (asking for a drink), we have a legal framework (in many countries you can't serve alcohol to minors), internal regulatory framework (in this company Gin Tonic should be served in a high foot round glass) and a cultural context (although legally it is forbidden to serve alcohol to minors, we serve anyone who pays for the drink).

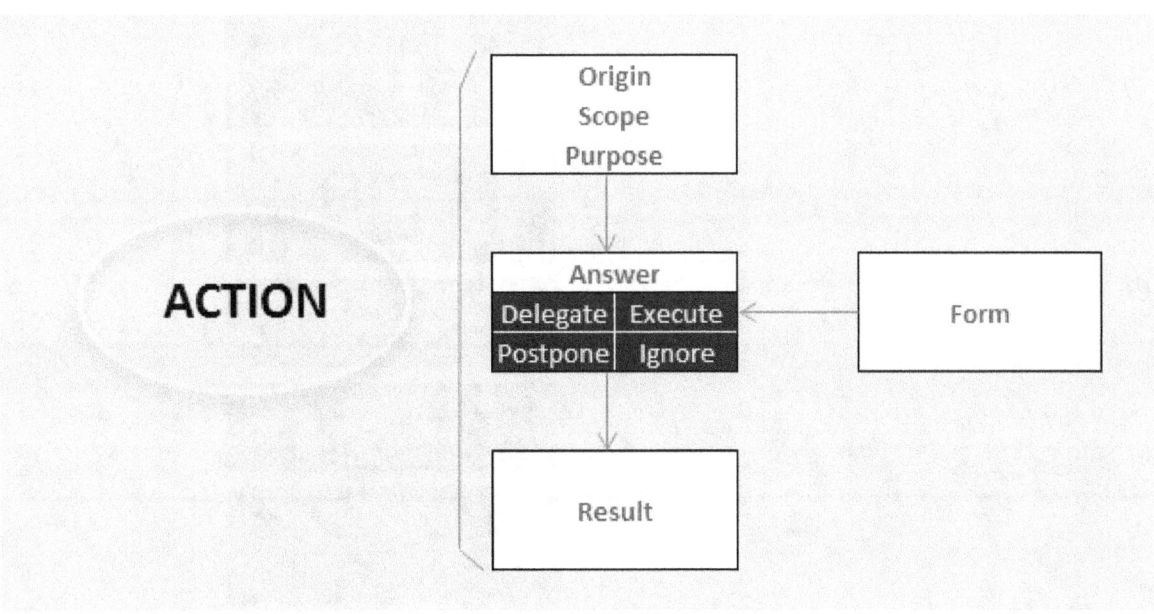

Figure 55 - Action idiosyncrasy

This action is developed with a purpose: to serve the customer, satisfying customer needs, making a profit, etc., and takes a particular form inherent to the execution (the task form, email, phone call, voice instruction, sending message through an intermediary, etc).

The action has a result.

The result is rarely fully comprehended. In our example, the drink may even have surpassed customer expectations and he does not show appreciation towards the company because, although satisfied, the customer may not request another immediately.

In an organization, actions are developed in the context of dependency relationships inherent to the task itself. We can observe actions that depend on a hierarchical authorization, actions which are operationally dependent on other people or departments, or even actions in which the worker is perfectly independent to execute them.

Simply sending an e-mail is an example of a situation of operational dependence. If the computer is not functional the action cannot be performed.

The frequency with which an action is performed, and the outbreaks of conflict that may arise, are important aspects for managing the company. It is helpful to identify situations where taking action is necessary and understanding redundancies, discouragement and difficulties, while performing the tasks.

In order to fully understand the company's practices, we will have to understand these aspects.

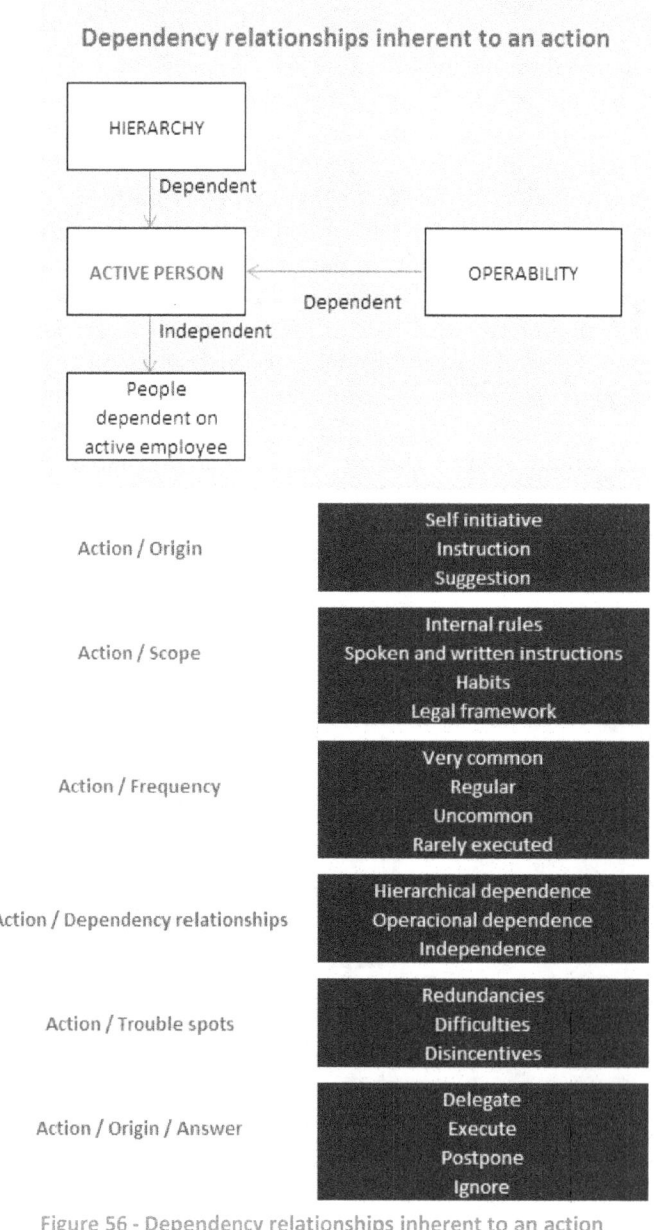

Figure 56 - Dependency relationships inherent to an action

My proposal to identify redundancies during execution has to do with the negative consequences that it may bring to the organization.

For example, if the owner of a bar orders a servant to put a set of dishes in a cardboard box after ordering another employee to arrange these same dishes in a cabinet, we may be facing a redundant action. One action may be excused because, apparently, the first worker could get the dishes in the cupboard at once.

The existence of redundant actions often lead employees to lower levels of implementation, and adoption of negative attitudes, such as "Why do I have to do this if someone will do that after me?".

By eliminating redundant actions, we can reduce costs and achieve productivity gains.

The parameters I propose must be adapted to the needs of each company. The choice of parameters should be made depending on the significance they have for the organization.

If we are aware of the information that we get, we can move on to developing a way for collecting information.

I propose something like this:

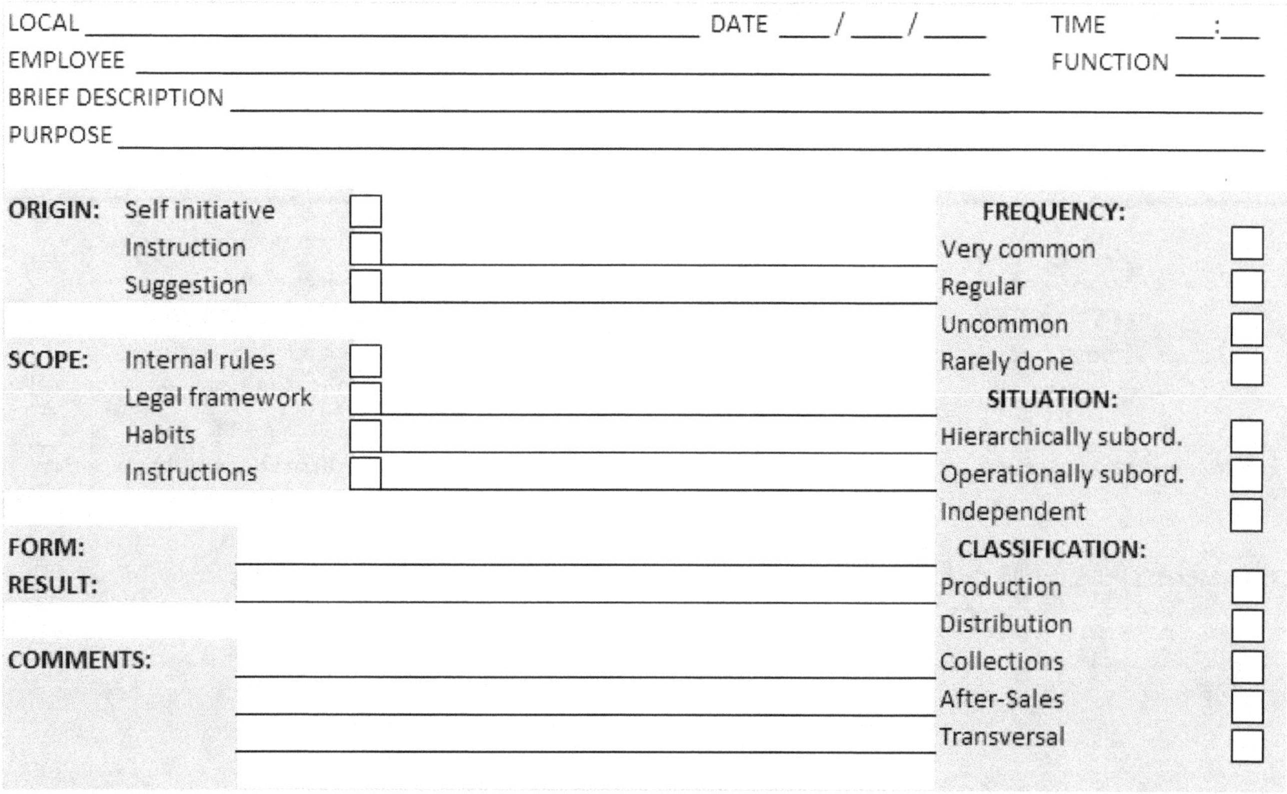
LOCAL ________ DATE ___/___/___ TIME __:__
EMPLOYEE ________ FUNCTION ______
BRIEF DESCRIPTION ________
PURPOSE ________

ORIGIN: Self initiative ☐ / Instruction ☐ / Suggestion ☐

SCOPE: Internal rules ☐ / Legal framework ☐ / Habits ☐ / Instructions ☐

FORM: ________
RESULT: ________

COMMENTS: ________

FREQUENCY: Very common ☐ / Regular ☐ / Uncommon ☐ / Rarely done ☐

SITUATION: Hierarchically subord. ☐ / Operationally subord. ☐ / Independent ☐

CLASSIFICATION: Production ☐ / Distribution ☐ / Collections ☐ / After-Sales ☐ / Transversal ☐

Figure 57 - Form example

A form of this kind is simple and intuitive in its presentation. When you are filling it, it doesn't involve the allocation of too much time for employees.

Filling in the "Comments" field should be requested whenever there are suggestions for improvement, identifiable sources of conflict inherent to an action, or when there is information about the origin of the action.

For example, stating that this is an action that was requested a few days ago and only now was executed.

We could get something like this at first:

LOCAL ___EP_____ DATE _2014_ / _04_ / _22_   TIME   _14:_30_

EMPLOYEE ___José Rodrigues_____   FUNCTION _Sales._

BRIEF DESCRIPTION __Submit a rebate request for "ABC" product_____

PURPOSE __Close a sale: client "XYZ Lda"_____

ORIGIN:	Self initiative	[X]		FREQUENCY:	
	Instruction	[ ]		Very common	[ ]
	Suggestion	[ ]		Regular	[X]
				Uncommon	[ ]
SCOPE:	Internal rules	[ ]		Rarely done	[ ]
	Legal framework	[ ]		SITUATION:	
	Customs	[X] Commercial structure		Hierarchically subord.	[X]
	Instructions	[ ]		Operationally subord.	[X]
				Independent	[ ]
FORM:	Email			CLASSIFICATION:	
RESULT:	Waiting for reply			Production	[ ]
				Distribution	[X]
COMMENTS:				Collections	[ ]
				After-Sales	[ ]
				Transversal	[ ]

Figure 58 - Form example, situation 1.1

On its own initiative, seller José Rodrigues requests a rebate via e-mail in order to complete the sale. He regularly performs this action, under his supervisor responsibility, and depending on information technology. This action is classified under product distribution, and is in accordance with the habits of the business structure of the company.

Since the result of this action depends on another set of actions, it is linked to them within the company.

A successive analysis of these forms helps us to perceive the kind of response that the company has in different dependent relationships between employees.

If there are a few more forms that request the same type of response from other employees, this will have a particular significance for the organization.

Where there are repeated requests by the same employees, which are chained to the first action, we may be facing an inability to provide the appropriate response to business needs.

LOCAL ___EP	DATE _2014_ / _04_ / _23_	TIME	_10:_40	
EMPLOYEE ___José Rodrigues		FUNCTION _Sales.__		
BRIEF DESCRIPTION __Verify if the discount was authorized				
PURPOSE __Understand if the discount was authorized for closing the deal with customer "XYZ Ltd"				

ORIGIN:				**FREQUENCY:**	
	Self initiative	☐		Very common	☐
	Instruction	☐		Regular	☐
	Suggestion	X	XYZ's contact informed they did wish to decide	Uncommon	☐
				Rarely done	X
SCOPE:	Internal rules	☐		**SITUATION:**	
	Legal framework	☐		Hierarchically subord.	☐
	Customs	X	Commercial structure	Operationally subord.	☐
	Instructions	☐		Independent	X
FORM:	Check e-mail and establish telephone contact			**CLASSIFICATION:**	
RESULT:	E-mail unanswered and unable to get telephone contact			Production	☐
				Distribution	X
COMMENTS:	This is rarely done because the person who is in charge			Collections	☐
	usually contacts anyone who requests			After-Sales	☐
	authorization.			Transversal	☐

Figure 59 - Form example, situation 1.2

If, in a succession of actions, the employee that triggered the first action now holds this form, the need for a second action rarely happens.

If this same employee had noted that the second action was "very common", then the analysis of the consequences would be significantly different, in terms of its occurrence, for the organization.

Forms must be built with a combination of simplicity and depth.

Simple to use, so that employees do not lose much time in their completion and can, without neglecting their normal duties, collaborate actively, seeking to register any action for a certain period of time, that is deemed appropriate (at least a week).

The depth of the information given to us, by the perception of the parameters of the action itself, will then allow us to group the information by department, by frequency and by dependence or independence degree.

Within each group of information, we can analyze the origin, response types, scope, form, and potential sources of conflict of an action.

Collecting, grouping and analyzing information are needed in order to meet the first two steps of the SIS-Structured Information Support building method: identifying needs and understanding the actions taking place at the company in a given period of time.

How to group information?

We can Group by:

- Value (frequency of occurrence x value = action value for the company);
- Dependent relationships (let's see how a chain of actions affects the organization);
- Form (format and / or media used that can detect opportunities to increase productivity and / or cost reduction);
- Departments (allows one to understand which actions are taking place in each area of the company).

We should look at the group of information without intending to make value judgments of any nature. It is only intended to identify where are the opportunities for improvement that represent greater value for the company, and what are the best ways to implement them.

In this building stage of the SIS, the information analysis is done in order to understand the actions that are developed within each group.

Understanding:

- Key people (the origin of the action?);

- Context (threat detection of serious errors and/or situations of lack of preparation, etc.);
- Response types (it means understanding the information collected if the response to the actions lie mainly in the delegation of action, immediate execution, delay in the action, or ignore the action that was required);
- Sources of conflict (it means to understand, by way of the collected information, which outbreaks of conflict exist and/or latent, and the impact of their occurrence in the organization).
- Why is it done?
- How is it done?
- Which levels of effectiveness?
- What affects effectiveness levels?

Consider for example a seller of a large company whose job description states:
"The employee's role is as follows:
(…)
i)   Contact existing and potential customers to promote sales of our products;
(…)"

The sellers of the company will contact your customers through personal contact, telephone, e-mail and through social networks. Perhaps the future will bring us an even greater diversity of possible means of contact.

Each employee will act in a certain way, giving preference to a means of contact over others.

Especially in meetings between management and middle management of large companies, results are often questioned (usually the highest incidence occurs over results below the desired targets), and the explanations given by middle management employees sound, almost always, as excuses…

Often, neither the Administration, nor the middle managers, truly understand the company itself!

In this example, the correct answer to the question "What is the optimal number of sellers?", clearly depends on how the tasks are carried out.

The process of understanding the information collected has to be analyzed by those who are experienced in the business.

It should include the largest possible number of prospects, because people have different visions of what impacts different actions within the company.

If business management has a certain view, there may be a different view for financial management, another different one for the direction of marketing, another for the legal services, and another for the IT services, and so on…

Each of these different perspectives is as valid as the other, and it is necessary to seize the different points of view, in order to build solutions that best serve the collective interest.

The involvement of these perspectives, with discretion and harmony, in the construction of the SIS, will enable the development of convergent thinking, strengthening the sense of "one for all, all for one", and extolling the individual sense of belonging to the organization.

Understanding the actions of the company helps management:
- Understanding the results;
- Recruiting people with the right profile (both in terms of their knowledge and in terms of their behaviors);
- Taking correct decisions when changing processes, basing these decisions on facts, instead of assumptions or individual perceptions (often biased by the individual perspective).

When there is a malfunction in an area of the company, this malfunction affects the performance of other areas, whether directly or indirectly, and this impact is not always easy to understand.

Currently, managers are increasingly looking at final results, after a certain length of time, without regard to the professional context in which these results occurred.

The possibility of making wrong decisions increases exponentially when a deep understanding of the actions undertaken by the company does not exist. The greatest danger to the organization arises when the difficulty in identifying the unorganized area can lead the direction of the company to make incorrect structural changes in areas which are properly organized in the company, which have just recorded results below what was desired. Meanwhile, its effectiveness is severely compromised by other areas of the organization of which this area is operationally dependent.

When companies have a well-implemented service model, based on the structured information support mechanism that defines the procedures for proper development of each action, inherent to different professional functions, the functions of top management are facilitated.

From the collection, grouping and analysis of information, we have identified the needs and understood the actions. It is now necessary to standardize practices.

The importance of the standardization of practices

When workers perform their tasks the same way, allocating equal amounts of time and material resources for the same tasks, the manager can clearly identify difficulties and find ways of simplifying the implementation of tasks.

At the same time, given the better understanding of how actions are developed, it is also common to identify opportunities for actions to be performed when taking into account competitor's weaknesses, whose exploitation can significantly increase the effectiveness of the team's actions.

If the leader of a working group identifies mechanisms to simplify the execution of tasks, he/she can also finds ways to increase productivity, which are usually accompanied by cost reduction.

Now consider the possibility of not being able to provide clear guidance when employees are performing their duties.

In this scenario, each employee makes things a hundred percent his/her way and different employees may get different records of productivity at the same time. Is the head of the working group in position to identify why this is happening? Is he able to explain why employee "A" has been successful, and employee "B" fell short of the target? What concrete actions can be done to promote the improvement of the collective results?

Without clear guidance as to how the tasks should be developed, you cannot have an effective coordination of collective effort, nor be effective when identifying mechanisms to simplify tasks that promote productivity increase and savings throughout the organization.

This raises the question: how to define clear guidance?

We currently live in a world in which large companies focus their operational processes on optimization. They appoint hierarchical superiors who are driven to exercise pressure over their subordinates towards getting results. They identify objectives, and let much of the definition of processes and tasks to be done by respective departments.

These organizations are self-limited to the capacity of individuals who serve the organization. These companies will live moments of euphoria, only when the circumstances allow the workers to find individual solutions to achieve the results defined at the beginning of each time period (which is usually one year). Characteristically, these are companies that vulgarize the use of commercial campaigns in short time periods, continuously promoting extraordinary sales efforts, but neglecting how these results are obtained.

When the results appear below target, managers will have an absolutely natural tendency to question the competence of each employee for the performance of their duties.

The fundamental question in these cases is: "What can be done to improve the results?". In this reality, the natural response is… to change employees!

When companies are facing realities similar to what was described, with a meager definition of execution processes and an almost exclusive focus on achieving results, they usually accompany this with a relatively high turnover of people in the exercise of those functions. The poor stability of people in their functions, combined with a low focus on the way things are done, inevitably results in lower quality of production, with negative effects that will be felt sooner or later in productivity levels of the organization.

In athletics, we have sprinters, middle distance athletes and marathon runners. In business, each employee also has his/her own characteristics and a smaller or larger virtue to perform certain tasks. Often, people ask a person with sprinters' characteristics to run a marathon, and then wonders about the end result without understanding how the person addressed the race…

When you do not provide clear guidance on how you intend tasks should be operationalized, each employee will do things a hundred percent his/her way. In this context, employees will feel that the results that were obtained depending of them, to a large percentage. There is room for developing a feeling such as "The company needs me…".

When there is clear guidance as how actions/tasks are intended to be done, the individual feeling that builds up will be closer to the idea that: "The company needs me to do this.".

In this sense, the sentimental relationship between workers and the company becomes more rational, controlled and, perhaps, even healthier.

Standardize practices

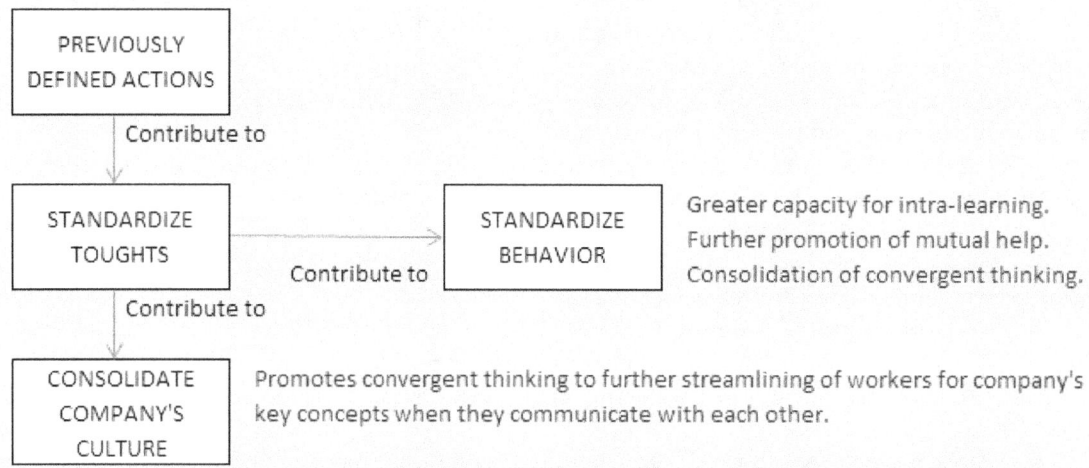

Figure 60 - Standardize practices

To standardize practices by providing clear guidance to employees, we need to define:
- The procedures;
- The time devoted to the task;
- Material resources;
- Human resources.

The standardization of actions in the company is critical to enable access to simplification processes for the company's management; leaving out being confined to the usual optimization processes.

Through understanding individual actions, individual creativity will allow employees to find mechanisms to improve the efficiency of their tasks, with consequent increases in productivity, often with cost reductions associated, increasing the overall efficiency of the company, as we shall see.

In parallel, the service's quality is improved and the ability to make a correct characterization of human resources needed for each function will be based on specific criteria and objectives.

The sprinter will compete in races of 100 and 200 meters. The middle-distance runner will run the 3,000 and 5,000 meters. The marathon runner will do the marathons.

This phase of the construction of the "SIS - Structured Information Support" can be facilitated by the choice of the physical storage where the information will be available.

The information can stay in:
- Digital support;
- Paper support;
- A fixed notice;
- Other media…

Nowadays, with the help of information technology, we have the information in digital form which is accessible almost anywhere in the world, with almost total freedom of mobility and access. The word "almost", here assumes great importance in the sense that there may be specific operational contexts stipulating the use of a different physical support to access information.

In general, for a better construction, implementation and usage, a digital support has greater prominence over other options we can consider.

Do information technologies help or hinder?

We may have the information available in e-mails, social networks, internet sites, intranet sites (exclusive network of the organization), public folders, CD's, DVD's, tablets, etc.

The information may be in intuitive, or on a format that is difficult to use.

The software tool can have many buttons and features, and no one knows how to use it. It may have a slow or quick interface, and be reliable, or can always be "crashing down".

The paper can be easily consulted and handling. And what about the ease of updating and disclosure?

Fixed notices may be easily consulted. And what can we conclude about its handling, updating, disclosure and suitability?

In short, the choice of support has to take into account the context in which this information will be used.

You should take into consideration if the use of this information is concentrated, or widely spread. Preferably, it should be as concentrated as possible.

The concentration of information in a single digital support, intuitive, simple to use and with easy access, is usually the more efficient, and natural choice, in response to the needs of the organization.

When designing this tool, we start from the groups we have and the "n" actions that are performed in the company and then start identifying walkthrough practices which are intended to be followed within the organization.

It is desirable that no action happens in the company without it being defined in the SIS - Structured Information Support.

Using the example presented at the beginning of the book, we can structure the information as expressed in the following page, according to the organization's own internal classification, with regard to the various departments.

This structure permits quick and intuitive access to information, which also works very well whenever a worker wants to deepen his/her knowledge about the procedures to be adopted in the different circumstances that may arise daily, reducing training needs, and promoting communication between employees beyond the most basic operational aspects. Instead of just asking the colleague "Where's the hammer?", the worker will be able to ask "Apart from hammering, do you use the hammer in other situations?".

This aspect is very important for fostering productivity gains. The time that each person has mentally available for others, is limited. A worker asks a question to a colleague, and probably gets an answer. If you pose two questions, possibly the second answer is evasive, because your colleague will no longer have the same patience that he/she had initially.

With an table of this kind before us, we can begin to identify the cells where the various actions taken previously, will fit.

	Production	Distribution	Collections	Post-Sale
Product line 1				
Product line 2				
Product line 3				
:				
:				
Product line N				

TRANSVERSAL	
Auditing	
Human resources	
Legal Services	
Accounting	
Logistics	
IT Department	
Quality	
Marketing	
Finances	

Figure 61 - Bidimensional table

At this point in the process, our puzzle is being built quickly…

Within each cell, we identify the key items where a response is necessary, so that actions can be developed, identifying the functions, the people, legal frameworks, internal standards, supporting documents, frequently asked questions, tips and procedures, and other aspects which are deemed relevant.

The procedures must define the way it is supposed to be done, the time devoted to the task, the person responsible and the person or people to whom the action is directed to.

	Production	Distribution	Collections	Post-Sale
Product line 1				
Product line 2				
Product line 3				
:				
:				
Product line N				

. Department
. Function
. Responsible
. Employees / Function / Contact
. Technical characteristics
. Sales Rhetorics
. Sales procedures
. Recovery procedures
. Post-sale procedures
. Raw material purshasing procedures
. Production procedures
. Supporting documentation
. Applied standards
. Delegated powers
. Legal framework

TRANSVERSAL	
Auditing	
Human resources	
Legal Services	
Accounting	
Logistics	
IT Department	
Quality	
Marketing	
Finances	

Figure 62 - Tridimensional table 1

In this example, I propose a set of items related to the "Product Line 2".
For each department of the company, we may have something like this:

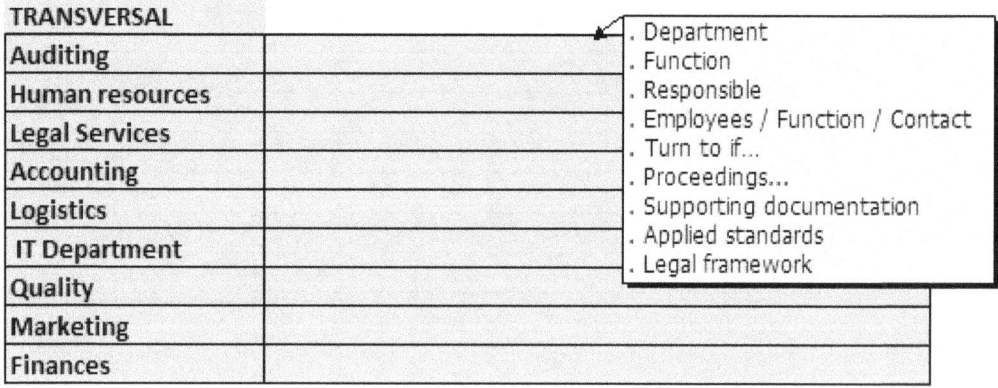

	Production	Distribution	Collections	Post-Sale
Product line 1				
Product line 2				
Product line 3				
:				
:				
Product line N				

. Department
. Function
. Responsible
. Employees / Function / Contact
. Turn to if...
. Proceedings...
. Supporting documentation
. Applied standards
. Legal framework

TRANSVERSAL	
Auditing	
Human resources	
Legal Services	
Accounting	
Logistics	
IT Department	
Quality	
Marketing	
Finances	

Figure 63 - Tridimensional table 2

In specific cases, there are certain actions which people may or may not be able to access due its condition – certain procedures can be conditioned by access levels previously determined, or delegated powers, keeping this information with a restricted and / or confidential character.

At this time, our tool is ready for consultation. Any action usually performed by an employee of the company can be consulted. Anyone can point out, accurately, the single and correct procedure, in a unique and precise way to anybody.

We want to ensure the principle of Security and Confidence, while performing the tasks. If people know the correct way of doing things and if this formula is well understood throughout the organization they will feel secure when executing their functions.

This tool does not yet foresee which of the correct procedures to apply in the event of unexpected scenarios.

Managing the unexpected

The management of unanticipated events is something that is rarely covered in the manuals of many organizations.

When an unforeseen event arises, by its nature, it poses a problem that needs a creative solution. The solution needs to address an answer to that difficulty, which in the case of an unforeseen, has created a context of action for which there are no adequate procedures previously defined.

Given such need, the employee will have one of four types of responses before the origin of an action:

- Delegate responsibility: Situation in which the worker comes to the aid of another person to find the solution. May be the case of a subordinate who decides that the responsibility of this solution lies within his/her hierarchical leadership, or, one hierarchical leader who is ordering a subordinate to find a solution to the problem, or even an employee who enlists the help of another colleague to solve this difficulty;
- Perform trouble-shooting: Situation in which the employee finds his/her own solution to the problem and puts it into practice;
- Postpone the solution: Situation where the worker decides he/she needs some time to find the best solution, and will collect additional information, that allows him/her to make a decision;
- Ignoring the problem: Situation where the worker decides that he/she will do nothing, because he/she does not want the responsibility for any kind of solution, or because he/she understands that the lack of resolution of the problem will not affect him.

Whenever the unexpected arises and is ignored, the company loses!

It loses an opportunity to strengthen the structure with an example of a surprising event that may occur again in the future. It also loses an opportunity for enhancing communication, and exchange of internal experiences.

It loses the opportunity to find a solution that may be useful for the whole organization in the future.

One should not allow an unforeseen event to be ignored, because that is the response that prevents the whole progress of the organization.

Whenever the unexpected arises, in the case of a situation that is not in the SIS - Structured Information Support, the employee must fill the action form, the kind that forms the basis for gathering information to build the SIS, so that we can analyze the situation, and decide on the disclosure of the solution across the enterprise.

Do not ignore the unexpected; its solution can be delegated or performed.

In any case, the form should always be filled, in order to collect information on the actions of the company.

If the situation, and / or the found solution, demonstrates being specific to a situation which is very localized in time, space and context, we can conclude that there is no need to mirror the solution in the SIS, but recording its occurrence is essential and the decision of its inclusion in the SIS should fit the higher hierarchical structures of organization.

But the first step when managing the unforeseen is the definition of unforeseen.

The company should consider any problem that lacks an answer that is not included in the SIS as unforeseen.

When someone needs to perform an action whose procedures are not defined, each employee will continue to provide the answer he wants to the problem and, ultimately, the leadership of the organization can feel the erosion of collective identity, when encountering the mischaracterization of the company.

For any cell in the SIS table, a rubric should be created called "In an unforeseen event..." which should set:
- Who is responsible for finding a solution?
- After filling the actions form (which gathers information) what follows?
- What is the maximum period of time in which the process should be completed?
- How will the implemented solution be disclosed and archived?

The mechanism guarantees that there is a development of a process of continuous learning within the organization, rooted in internal communication, in the search for creative solutions and improvement of processes.

Real life is sneaky and will sabotage your plans when you least expect it

An example of this are transitional situations.

The rules may be well defined, the entire company may be converging around a particular line of thought, when an exception arises…

Consider for example a situation where physical facilities of an operating unit are changed. In this process, the operation unit is compromised. Consequently, their ability to perform the tasks that were assigned will necessarily be affected in multiple aspects, along with the relationship with other departments of the company.

The most common solution for most companies is to do nothing in a different way. Sometimes, one thinks of returning to normality as soon as possible, and does not consider what he/she should do differently during the transition process.

The accumulation of problems will be higher as the transition process is in full swing. When what was intended to be temporary is prolonged in time, the consequences can be catastrophic!

The company's management cannot accept that there are sabotaging processes in the normal operation of the organization.

Any temporary, transient and / or specific situation, conferring a state of abnormality to the operation of the organization, needs one of the two steps:
- Either it is included in SIS - Structured Information Support;
- Or it will be treated according to the rules defined for "Unexpected" Management.

Thus, this will ensure the safeguarding of an effective control over the actions that are developed everyday by the top management of the company.

We get significant increases of information that is available for analysis, and gains of objectivity in decision making, leaving less and less situations up for decisions which are made by chance.

The principle of Safety and Confidence is enhanced because the actions before an unforeseen event happen suitably managed by a set of predetermined procedures.

Implementation

In my mind, the implementation of SIS - Structured Information Support should be made taking into account the previously established communication with all employees about this tool.

However, at this point, it is absolutely relevant to recapitulate all stages that were developed to date while building the SIS, explaining that the final definition of procedures is the result of the collection, grouping, analysis and standardization of practices already in used in the company.

There is not really anything new. It consists only in giving concrete shape to the global set of actions that are already developed together, allowing the company to obtain gains in productivity and communication within the company.

It is important to communicate that there is an added responsibility applied to all: the proper execution of tasks. It is also a responsibility of the company management to regularly check the proper functioning of the organization in accordance with what is established.

Then, we inform employees in detail on how the information was organized, where it is available for consultation, and outline the proper procedures for "unforeseen" management, which is absolutely crucial for the consistency of this tool over time.

At last, it matters to mention how any changes that may be implemented in the SIS- Structured Information Support in the future should be disseminated and implemented.

SIS's Implementation

Explain to the whole company that this mechanism:

1- Final Result = $\sum$ (Picking, grouping, analysis and standardization) of already existing practices;

2- Enables gains in productivity and communication;

3- Promotes greater collective responsibility on task execution;

4- Encourages the organization of information and contingency management procedures;

5- Any future changes to SIS will be disclosed.

Figure 64 - SIS's implementation

Maintenance

Once deployed, the maintenance of the SIS - Structured Information Support becomes extremely simple, since the management mechanism of the unexpected/unforeseen is well defined.

Like any other procedure, the very action of amendment and maintenance of SIS should be defined at the outset, particularly how to do it, the time devoted to the initiation and completion of the task, the material resources used and the human resources involved (who is responsible for doing what).

The maintenance of SIS implies an active and continuous vigilance on the part of the company's management. In a larger organization, this responsibility can, and should, be delegated to the person responsible for quality control, which, by virtue of these functions, needs to be someone with power to act next to the one who performs the physical changes in the SIS.

For any chosen support (usually the digital), the person responsible for managing the SIS has to maintain a close connection to those who perform physical changes in the chosen support, so that there are no large gaps of time between the need and the implementation of amendments, ensuring that the tool actually it is very useful in day-to-day business.

Conclusion

With a SIS- Structured Information Support anchored in the daily practice of the company, the analysis of variances recorded between results and targets it is likely to be explained by identifying those that have demonstrated a lower efficacy.

Actions may have been poorly executed, may be inappropriate to the context where they were developed; insufficient in the face of competition action, etc.

On the other hand, actions that may have been particularly well executed, extremely appropriate and that have occurred within a context of anticipation (over competition), ultimately will be noted.

In addition to the operational benefits above and beyond the communication gains within the organization, with the construction of SIS - Structured Information Support, the company's management acquires a tool that is made to aid the decision making process that increases the accuracy when identifying needs of amendment (people's level or processes' level).

Cumulatively, their regular use creates conditions for continuous internal learning, to the development of convergent thinking, and for valuing the feeling of belonging to the organization.

Then check where your organization is located…

Structured Information Suport				
Level 5: Continuously improve	The sources and frequencies of the problem are documented as part of work routine, the root problems are identified and corrective action plans are developed.	The Structured Information Support is also used to facilitate the work among colleagues. Mutual help manifests itself increasingly within the company.	There are responses to stimuli that extend beyond the role of the worker, and are given in an unique and convergent manner across the enterprise. There is a growing sense of belonging to the organization.	The management of unforeseen developments is naturally assumed. Each occurrence is documented and involves the largest possible number of areas in the organization.	The SIS is continually conceived towards its improvement (simplification and optimization), aiming at the highest possible efficiency in the context in which it is engaged.
Level 4: Focus on reliability	The frequency of actions and their impact in terms of costs and benefits are reviewed periodically based on the inherent value to the organization.	The knowledge of the business practices extends beyond the individual tasks of each employee. The SIS is referenced in the communication between people.	The responses to stimuli and the execution of actions happen naturally, according to the recommendations in the SIS. People feel safe and confident while executing tasks.	Reliable methods of solving unforeseen events are properly documented and are followed by the entire workgroup.	The Structured Information Support is unique and easy to access. There is a method for the way that internal standards are published by the organization and how information is updated.
Level 3: Make it visual	an information structured support is created for easy reference and general access, used for training, and guidance in the performance of tasks.	The know-how, the time devoted to the task and the human and material resources involved are known. Practices are developed evenly.	The execution of actions is appropriate and the same happens about task delegation. Postpone actions and ignored stimuli rarely arise. People feel confident in their roles.	Each worker confines the defined procedures correctly in the event of unforeseen circumstances, including the occurrence report and inner registration.	The working group ensures the continuous verification of procedures as defined in the Structured Information Support.
Level 2: Focus on basics	The information regarding the action is collected, analyzed, understood and worked according to their value to the company.	The company has defined homogenous practices. Situations of functional dependency are considered in the performance of tasks.	The execution of actions is appropriate to the stimulus. There is still an inappropriate delegation of tasks. Postpone action and ignored stimuli arise occasionally.	Each worker knows the procedures to follow and identifies the person responsible for the solution of an unforeseen problem.	Structured data means are chosen and the inherent methodology is defined along with its construction, update and leaders.
Level 1: Just beginning	There are multiple information means, with dissemination of instructions by voice, brochures, emails, manuals, etc.	Actions are developed independently and differ from individual to individual. Each worker performs many of his/her tasks in his own way.	Ignoring and postponing are the responses to various stimuli of action and there are too many situations of delegated tasks. People often feel unsafe in execution.	Often employees solve problems by themselves and are not working with any kind of procedure of the adopted solutions.	There isn't any single structured information support that is easy to access. There is no method for the way that internal standards are published by the organization.
Place yellow box where each area is on the ISS Levels of Achievement	**Information**	**Practical actions**	**Answers Feelings**	**Contingency management**	**Implementation Maintenance**

Figure 65 - Structured Information Support Levels

2.8 FOCUSED SIMPLIFICATION

Focused Simplification

Focused Simplification is a practice that seeks to explore the creativity of its employees in organizations.
When performed successfully, it results in a clear benefit for the company and for its customers.
The entire company makes a promise before it performs a service. This promise, in the customer's perspective, may or may not be fulfilled.

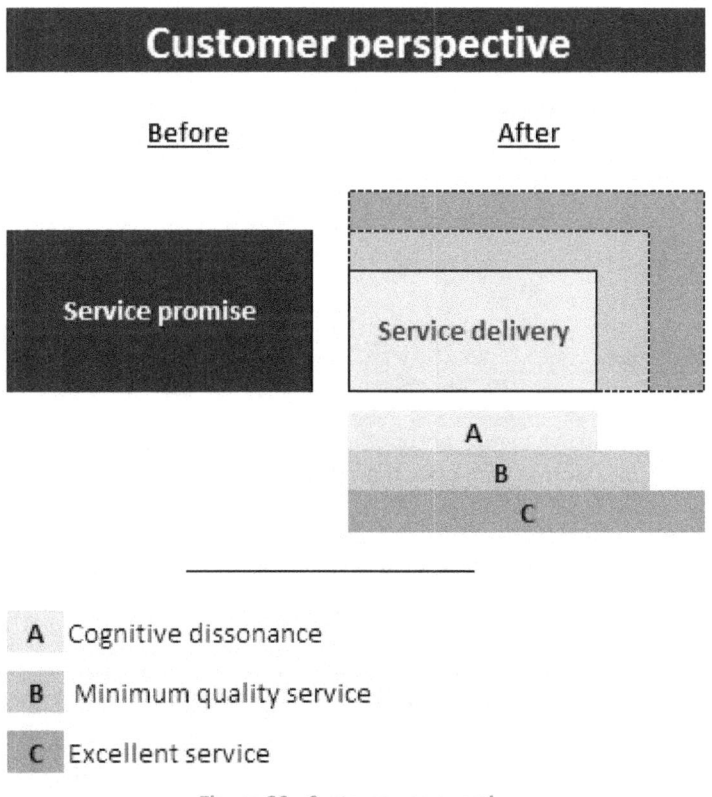

Figure 66 - Customer perspective

In "A", the level of service that is actually provided to the customer is perceived as being inferior to what was promised before purchase. There is a mismatch between the client's feelings of satisfaction, anticipated prior to purchase, and the feeling of satisfaction experienced after purchase. When faced with this kind of experience, the customer tends to seek the competition for his/her next purchase.

"B", in the customer's perspective, refers to the level of service provided which matches exactly the level of service expected before purchase. The customer feels satisfied that he got what he wanted, in accordance with the agreement between the parties.

In "C", the company positively surprised the client(s), exceeding their initial expectations. This is the kind of situation in which the client says with satisfaction: "Excellent!"

It is here that creativity makes the difference!

Creativity is something that should be present every day, during business activities, because you have to provide an excellent service without charging excessively for improvements.

People do not value the same experience in the same way, at the same time. Companies of excellence set their service standards such as company "B" and "C". Mediocre companies position themselves predominantly in "A".

Although there are a certain set of circumstances that may present temporary difficulties when trying to provide good service, there is room for employees to express their creativity, when companies really create conditions for a basic service either type "A" or "B", to be perceived by customers as a service type "B" or "C".

If we always do everything the same way, how can we surprise our clients?

The level of expression of individual creativity plays an important role in the organization's competitiveness.

In order for creativity to be fully explored in the organization, people have to feel they have freedom of expression to manifest themselves, but also feel that their ideas can be accepted.

Before stimulating creativity, we must liberate divergent thinking. We have to promote the creation of options within the organization, and encourage the emergence of the ideas to make things simpler.

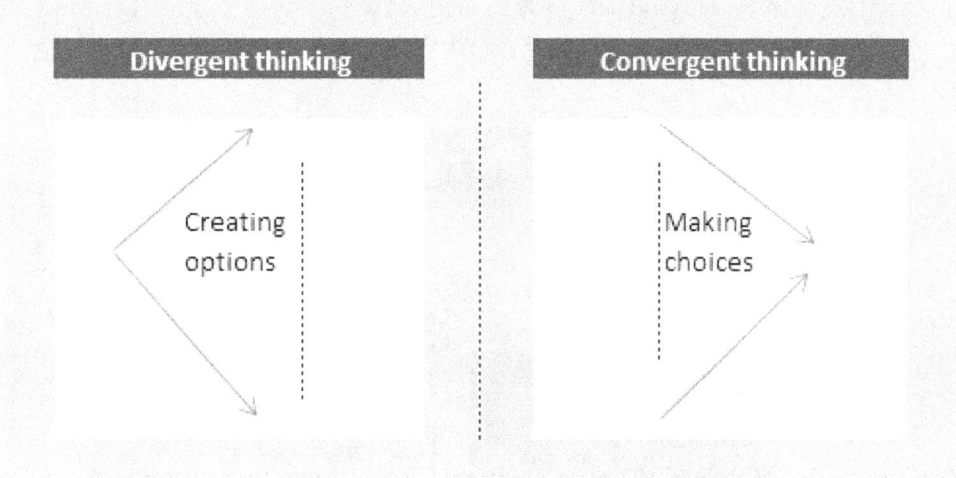

Figure 67 - Thinking, divergent vs convergent

While divergent thinking contains higher emotional burdens in itself, because it is closer to people's feelings, here, convergent thinking assumes dominance over the rational component, looking to find the best solutions to the problems that may arise.

Both are important. Both are influential. Both must be taken into account.

When James Wood Young wrote the book "A Technique for Getting Ideas", about a methodology for getting ideas, he defined fundamental principles and methods to succeed.

The principles are as follows:

1º The idea is a novel combination of old elements.

2º The ability to find novel combinations of old elements depends on the ability to detect relationships between things.

The first step in the idea generation method is the collection of raw materials, in general and specific terms. The last presupposes knowledge far beyond the surface, looking for the individuality of the relationships that lead to an idea.

The collection of material involves listening without underestimating the ideas of others. Observe without making value judgments. Be curious about "why" things are done a certain way. Reflect on the possibilities, without considering only one as being the correct one.

Yonathan Dominitz, entrepreneurial creativity guru and founder of Mindscapes (themindscapes.com), argues that inspiration and practicality have to follow their path by holding hands.

The practical realization of an idea requires us to separate the concepts of idea and innovation.

Creativity is an individual process. The idea arises in one's mind.

Innovation is a collective process. An idea which is discussed collectively leads to a change in perceptions.

While creativity is the idea itself, innovation is the realization of this idea.

In the business world, creativity is wasted a lot. Freedom to expose ideas to collective criticism is very rare and limited to the Marketing and Research and Development departments in the design of new products.

Often, there is a significant waste of the creative capacities of the remaining members of the organization.

In many companies we have seen the presence of specific rooms/support mechanisms for gathering suggestions from every employee.

What is important is that people feel confident to make a suggestion whenever they identify an opportunity for improvement, regardless of the position they hold in the company, without fear of criticism, and within a spirit of constructive commitment to the organization.

In order for this to happen, it is important to have dialogue and communication between the various sectors and areas of operation, so that associations and innovative combinations may arise as a result of several individual perspectives.

You cannot allow some personality aspects to interfere with any employee being able to give his input. The shy one or the quiet one can have suggestions and ideas that may be better than an extrovert person. They most probably think differently. And this difference of perspectives adds value to the company if all staff adds their opinion.

The way the suggestions are worked and grasped differs significantly from company to company.

How to value a long list of suggestions and decide which ones should be put into practice?

In many companies, this decision is confined to a narrow range of people, often near the top of the company. In these scenarios, the decision to implement suggestions inevitably passes through joining these suggestions with their own individual perspectives, thereby limiting the organization's performance.

This will not be the best way to enhance collective growth.

It is important that everyone, including the senior managers of the company, realize how much we are limited by our experiences. Our ability to see things can be amplified when we look at the different perspectives that others can bring to the table.

It is true that the deeper knowledge of the organization, inherent to certain functions, may bring a greater capacity for rational judgment in the decision making process, but this judgment should be made as much as possible, accepting the perspectives of others.

The practical evaluation of suggestions is a challenge for organizations.

When this evaluation is based on mutual respect when dealing with different individual perspectives, it is perhaps the main step and the key for enhancing individual creativity in favor of collective.

As mentioned earlier, the Focused Simplification is an engaging process for integrating people and constituent departments of an organization, in the pursuance of obtaining productivity gains in firms.

The simplification aims to find a solution to a given problem, which enables the attainment of the same end result with less effort.

The focus is on concentrating our energies on what is truly important: the ongoing task.

The FS - Focused Simplification consists in taking advantage of the diversity of perspectives intrinsic to individuals who make up the organization, using all their creative potential, according to business priorities.

When the process of FS - Focused Simplification is implemented, the company obtains significant gains in competitiveness, as a result of the concentration on the suggestions of their employees while solving individual and collective problems.

Inherent advantages:
- Cost reduction;
- Greater operational efficiency;
- Greater capacity for innovation;
- Higher Excellency levels, i.e., greater ability to surprise positively.

It presents some challenges:
- Ensuring the integration and involvement of all employees;
- Appreciate the suggestions presented by different individuals, with different perspectives, objectivity, and respect for differences, without making value judgments;
- Ensure the suggestions that are not implemented do not constitute any source of dissatisfaction to the employees who formulated them;
- Developing a methodology for collecting, processing and implementation of suggestions, as to ensure the effectiveness of the process.

"Simplicity is about subtracting the obvious and adding the meaningful."

John Maeda

With the creation of the Focused Simplification process, we intend to ensure the fulfillment of two fundamental principles:

1- Curiosity and Involvement
2- Dynamics and Efficiency

Curiosity and Involvement

When curiosity dominates our thinking, we seek to understand why are things done a certain way, and not just do whatever we want, just because it has always been done like this. When we perceive what is around us, we begin to be able to establish relationships between things, often finding unique and appropriate solutions to a given problem.

It is necessary that this curiosity is at the organization's service, fostering individual involvement of each employee in the FS process (FS-Focused Simplification).

Dynamics and Efficiency

If change is a constant situation in life, what is the value of stability?

Resistance to change is inherent to our natural fears, regarding the danger of the unknown. Resistance to change by employees is costly for organizations.

Antonio Damásio found that behind individual uniqueness there is stability.

Acquiring a momentum of progress involves the adoption of simplification procedures, by which the expression of individual creativity is exerted on a given reality known to all.

If the set of suggestions for simplification is evaluated according to a known methodology, respectful of different individual perspectives and aggregative of collective interests, the organization achieves significant gains in efficiency, meaning that it will implement the changes that are necessary in the circumstances presented, taking into account individual and collective interests.

The company can convert "interests in common" into "common interests".

The value of an individual suggestion depends on the benefit it brings to the collective.

Teamwork is has a dynamic inherent to the elements that constitute the team.

There are aspects, identified by several authors, which unambiguously characterize the dynamics of teamwork.

If the team works as a single body, then the following three premises will occur:

1- Participation is balanced – everyone has a place;
2- There is renunciation to individual positions (not to individual identity);
3- There is complementarity of individual capabilities.

When the team really works, its elements are considered collectively responsible among themselves, and do indeed feel that way.

There is true communication and dissenting opinions are encouraged.

Respect, open-mindedness, unity and cooperation, are consolidated values in the working group.

Participation and commitment are the basic principles of action.

Efficiency implies that there are no losses in the process for obtaining results. Consequently, there is a need for the company to have the ability to harness the latent potential in the working group.

We are trying to implement a collective dynamic of progress, funded by the constant search for efficiency, which is necessary for long-term consistency.

The principle of Dynamics and Efficiency is based on the recognition of the need to maintain a constant search for efficient improvement that is essential in the methodology of the Focused Simplification process.

Before actually advancing to the practical implementation of the method of Focused Simplification, it is useful to reflect about how companies have dealt with the creativity of its employees, recently.

Until the late twentieth century, companies had serious trouble with effectiveness.

Two aspects emerge as key constraints for the effectiveness of companies:

1- Sometimes the suggestions are inadequate, i.e., employees generally tend to make suggestions for improvement that result in immediate improvement of their own well-being, or suggestions that imply a critical load to the top management of the company. In both cases, it is acceptable that for the organization, it may not make sense to implement those suggestions.

2- Given the suggestion of a colleague, it is frequent to find another collaborator coming out with a counter-suggestion or amending it, which weakens the initial suggestion, usually generating unconstructive debate, which does not favor the company's productivity.

Recognizing the importance of harnessing the potential of existing creativity in business, coupled with pressure by gains in competitiveness, has led organizations to develop their own processes to collect new ideas, trying to do it in a controlled environment.

In this sense, the processes of "brainstorming" and "fast brainstorming" have been an increasing recourse.

In the "brainstorming" process, companies promote meetings concerning various topics among their employees, seeking the generation of innovative ideas (innovative ideas = creative ideas that can be put into practice) through employee debates.

These meetings are necessarily time consuming and have, inherently, a set of costs that are not always truly monetized by organizations.

Then, this situation evolves to the meetings of "fast brainstorming".

In "fast brainstorming" we gather simultaneously a wide range of collaborators to discuss key issues for the organization.

We split the large group into smaller groups, giving each small group a single theme.

One distributes rapidly a set of post-it notes for each element, and asks them to point out their suggestions to solve the problem (or seizing opportunities), related to the theme which your group is responsible for.

We collect the individual information, and group the four or five solutions that emerge as the most common, within each small group.

Then, we finally group together the collected information with respect to the four or five solutions that are to be implemented, and these final solutions are disclosed by all.

This process achieves a rapid spread (within the organization) of what seems to be the best practices pertaining to key issues for the company, presumably with greater productivity than what was found in "brainstorming." meetings.

In what concerns to the use of creativity, both processes have limitations that reveal its ineffectiveness:

"Brainstorming"   People are conditioned by aspects inherent to their personality. Not everyone expresses themselves publicly with the same foresight and will, and many feel inhibited to submit their suggestions, even when they believe their ideas are preferable to the existing ones.

People are conditioned by the existence of pressure to produce ideas.

"Fast brainstorming"   In addition, this process is also conditioned by the absence of dialogue and reduced sharing of experiences, often leaving a feeling of wasted time in participants (sometimes called "false brainstorming").

A good idea may be rejected simply for being in the minority, not even reaching a debate.

Ideas do not arise when we want to.

Good ideas come unexpectedly, after a period of mental processing of information that shapes them. They show up in the bath, while shaving, during a road trip, drinking coffee, looking at something, listening to music, etc.

Always carry something where you can save your idea… It might be a good idea! ☺

With the development and mass use of computing resources in organizations, the creation of an efficient process for collecting suggestions can truly harness the creative potential of enterprises.

The principles of "Curiosity and Involvement" and "Dynamics and Efficiency", must stand out so we can conclude that the process of Focused Simplification is preferable to the alternatives we have at the moment.

Let us turn over a challenging case study of managing a transportation public service, that helps us define the methodology for implementing the FS process (FS - Focused Simplification).

The manager of a regular bus service was responsible for the bus route on a small town by seaside.

Due to the uneven ground, buses just went in and out of the village by the same site.

There were two bus stops located in the village in order to equally divide the resident population, whether in terms of number of inhabitants or in terms of distance to walk to the bus stop.

These bus stops were properly authorized and negotiated with local authorities.

The bus was entering the town making the route shown on the map with the green line.

Passengers were collected at bus stop "A", followed by bus stop "B". The bus collected the passengers and returned by the same road, the only one adequate to the frequent road traffic.

Figure 68 - Focused simplification, case study 1

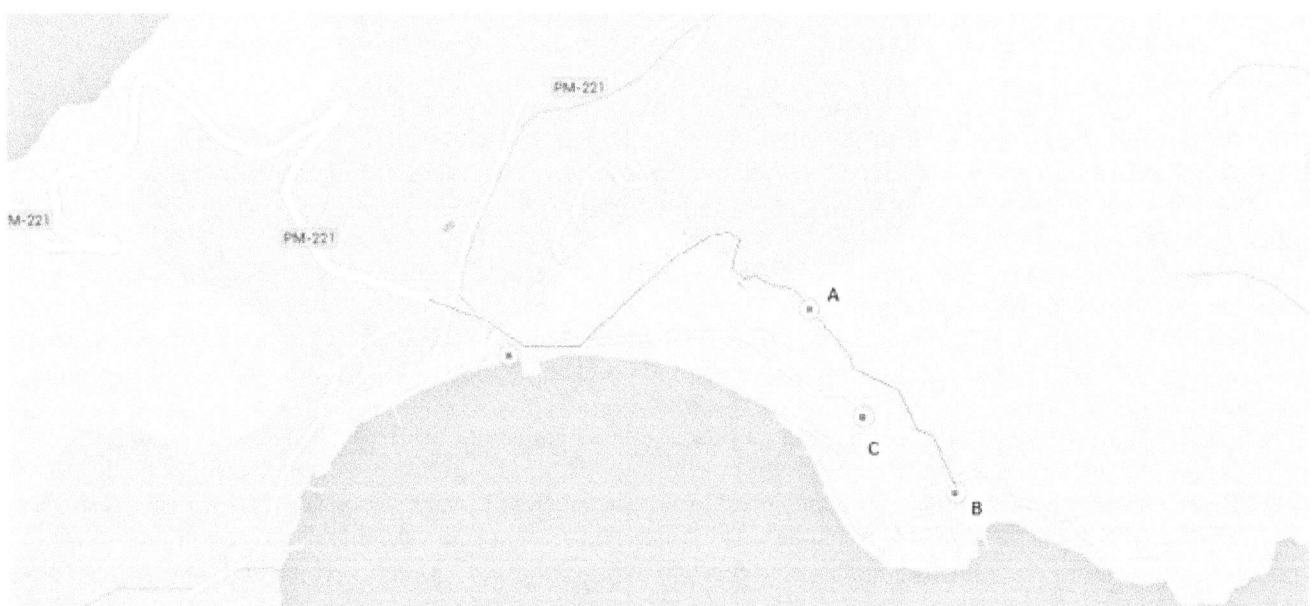

Figure 69 - Focused simplification, initial bus stop locations

One day, a resident of the village complained by writing to the company, suggesting the elimination of bus stop "B" and carry out a new bus stop at point "C".

He justified his request by stating that he would rather climb 100 meters of his residence to bus stop "C" than having to descend 500 meters to bus stop "B".

The manager of the regular bus service noticed at once that the source of the request was due solely to the personal convenience of a client.

What would be his decision?

Figure 70 - Focused simplification, case study 2

Here's what the manager did...

Analyzing from the standpoint of the company, the requested change didn't represent a significant change in terms of cost, since the suggested route was similar to the actual one.

In practical terms, it would require a license from the local power authorities to make the requested change.

He decided to raise an opinion survey among all passengers who used their public bus services in that village. Developed a simple information explaining that he was considering the possibility of changing the second bus stop from "B" to "C" and then requested that the passengers manifest themselves in favor or against , making sure that each passenger stated his/her opinion only once.

The drivers were instructed to carry out the collection of this information for a month.

Surprisingly, a month later, there were no objections towards the change in location and had gathered a percentage higher than 80% of votes in favor of the change.

The manager contacted the local authorities and requested the change of location of the second bus stop within the locality, justifying the request with the initial client request and the results of the specific survey developed for this purpose among the service users.

Figure 71 - Focused simplification, case study 3

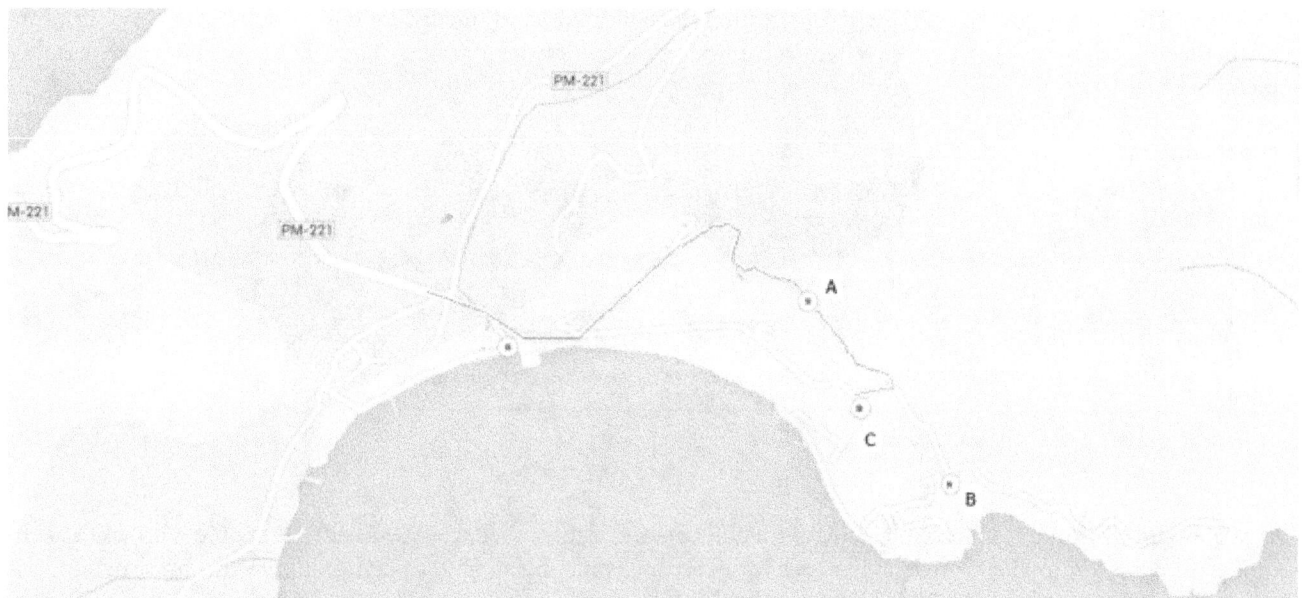

Figure 72 - Focused simplification, final bus stop locations

The "B" bus stop has been disabled and the buses route inside the city came up as indicated on the second map.

Curious, the manager asked the reason why no one filled an opposition to the deactivation of the bus stop at "B". He found out that this part of the city was inhabited by families who have become used to use their own car and lived in a larger residential housing type.

He concluded that the bus stop at "B" was much less useful than bus stop "C" and the location of the "C" point served the interests of a greater number of inhabitants residing in the village.

Figure 73 - Focused simplification, case study 4

The approach taken by the manager to the situation had several merits:
1- He defined the problem;
2- He addressed the problem while being free of prejudices, without necessarily considering initial location of the bus stops as correct: he observed the situation without making any value judgments;
3- He gathered additional information;
4- He contextualized the measures within the framework of operational efficiency in the business;
5- He verified and validated the results, concluding what was the best decision, for the interest of all.

When searching for the method itself, the approach for solving problems, typified in the scientific method, is also appropriate in this business context:
1- Problem definition;
2- Data collection;
3- Hypothesis formulation (suggestion);
4- Test or experience (validity check);
5- Conclusion (result analysis).

Similarly, the method for implementing the Focused Simplification process begins with the identification of the problem / opportunity, presents a possible suggestion for resolution / action, verifies efficiency criteria, validates the suggestion, and ends with setting up an action plan.

In relation to the scientific method itself, a period of data collection prior to the formulation of suggestions does not occur. The suggestion arises, then information is collected, and finally, one draws conclusions about its implementation. This conclusion is based on three clear efficiency criteria: advantage, benefit and ease of implementation.

Schematically:

Figure 74 - Focused simplification, implementation model

We intend to explore individual creativity for the benefit of the collective. We seek that people who work at the company find ways to make everyday life easier for everyone, while being able to communicate this information, and assuring that its implementation will be as soon as possible.

The most effective way to achieve this is by assuming that any suggestion should be implemented, and acting towards its implementation.

Only this way we can be genuine when accepting suggestions of others and making them a real possibility (of implementation/solution).

The implementation of the idea will always be conditioned by its feasibility and efficiency. Assuming that any suggestion should be implemented, this makes you truly consider the possibility of doing so. This attitude, in itself, constitutes a stimulus for all elements of the organization to be motivated to participate.

It constitutes an internal authorization, stating that the perspective of the company about things can change.

If the first step of the methodology is to assume that any suggestion should be implemented, the second step is to create an expeditious process of collecting and processing suggestions.

This process of collection and the processing of suggestions has to enhance and explore individual creativity.

To do so, suggesting the collection of ideas is not enough. It is also necessary to motivate the discussion of ideas. The difficulty is to do it in a practical way, and without compromising the productivity of the whole enterprise.

"The more simple we are, the more complete we become."

August Rodin

First things first. In this second step, we first have to get the idea. After that, we have to promote the discussion of the idea.

With the aid of computer tools, some companies already have a small form made for the purpose of collecting suggestions from its employees. Afterwards, it is analyzed by the responsible department, and conclusions regarding its implementation are established by the same department. Often, the debate concerning an idea is null or weak, whether in relation to the prospects considered, or to the involvement of other employees, who do not participate directly in the process, in the first place.

The greater or lesser involvement of the different constituent parts of the company depends directly on the decision of the first person, responsible for receiving the suggestion. The debate of ideas begins, at first, being conditioned by the "receiver", and the suggestion is then also limited by the number and functions of the people who comment such idea.

Apart from the decision maker, both in case of implementation as in case of rejection, there is rarely a clear perception of the staff in relation to "why" was implementation/rejection the final outcome.

When, within the companies, we encourage that a suggestion made by an employee is being subjected to debate, we achieve, almost immediately, an automated process for improvement of the initial suggestion.

Ideas are seldom born perfect. When subjected to debate, people constructively optimize the initial idea. The end result surpasses the sum of its parts.

Everyone makes their contribution.

Everyone feels that the end result has a little bit of them.

The third step of the methodology consists in obtaining the validation of the suggestion.

There must be a quick and expeditious objective analysis that can facilitate decision making regarding their implementation.

There are different perspectives one can use to analyze the same situation. This fact makes it advisable to get the opinion of all members of the organization and yields significant gains in creativity, objectivity and operability.

We should also seek the involvement of all people, with gains of communication within the organization. The Focused Simplification process is working as a process of promoting divergent thinking, based on the premise, "all for the common interest".

The validation of the suggestion is made in a practical way, based on three objective criteria:

- Advantage: positive effects on the organization;
- Benefit: cost reduction or income increases;
- Ease of implementation.

Each person in the company should decide, as to their perception, if a change is helpful by using each of these three criteria. For an employee of financial management, it may seem easy to implement the suggested changes, on the program for monitoring the customers' balance, as mentioned in the example "Signaling and controlling collections" (p. 40) and for the IT department, the same change may seem as virtually impossible to implement.

Each department has their own needs, difficulties, limits and constraints, which are not always perceived by colleagues from other areas of the company. If everyone states their opinions on a given suggestion, the top management of the company gets diverse and useful information, regarding the difficulties experienced simultaneously in several areas (the person who suggests improvements, the person arguing there are difficulties with implementation), and they are able to identify opportunities and / or potential ideas that exist and that are, perhaps, not being explored.

For each of the three criteria, employees have to examine the suggestion and deepen their analysis, as shown below:

1- Advantage: We may have…

    1.1 Material advantages;

    1.2 Operational advantages (improving the speed or quality of execution);

    1.3 Behavioral advantages (inducer of good practice).

2- Benefit: We may have benefits…

    2.1 By reducing costs;

    2.2 By increasing incomes.

3- Ease of implementation: We may achieve this or that by…

    3.1 Putting it into practice in a short time;

    3.2 Simplicity regarding technical resources needs;

    3.3 Simplicity regarding material resources needs;

    3.4 Simplicity regarding human resources needs.

If each employee gives his/her opinion based on these three criteria, by simply assigning a score of 1 to 5, decision making can be grounded, not only in what appears to be the needs of the company, but also in what is effectively the company's potential.

Often, the suggestions that are received and analyzed by a single decision maker are biased by the analyst's perspective and limited by his/her usual inability to have a global perception on the ease of each suggestion's implementation.

A valued suggestion ABE (5,5,5) for most workers should be given serious consideration within a company. It means that all employees consider it an **A**dvantageous suggestion for the organization, **B**enefic and of **E**asy implementation, without someone saying otherwise.

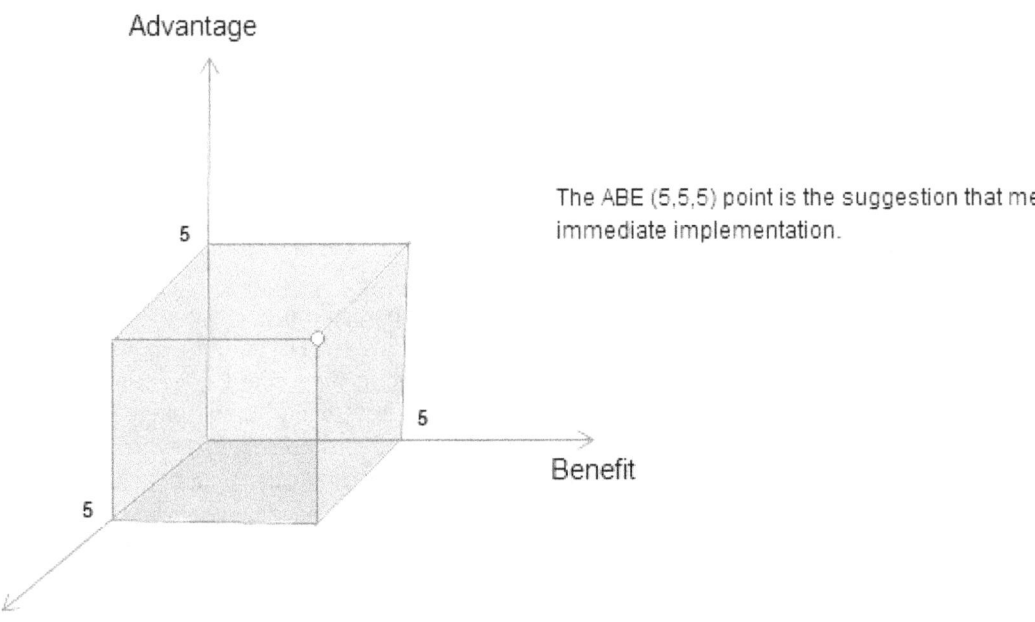

Figure 75 - Focused simplification, main criteria

The form (collection of suggestions) should be as simple as possible, so that filling it and understanding it can be user friendly and intuitive.

LOCAL _____ DATE ___ / ___ / ____ TIME ___:___
EMPLOYEE _____ FUNCTION _____

Problem/Oportunity
_____
_____
_____

Root problem? YES [ ] NO [ ]

Base suggestion
_____
_____
_____

Practical suggestion
_____
_____
_____

	1	2	3	4	5
Advantage					
Benefit					
Easy implementation					

Deadline for collecting opinions: ___ / ___ / ____
Completion date _____ : ___ / ___ / ____
Implementation date _____ : ___ / ___ / ____

Figure 76 - Focused simplification, form example

In this proposal, we can see that this initial form identifies the employee who makes the suggestion, the date of the suggestion, the problem or opportunity in question, the basis of such suggestion (or the solution advocated by the employee) and the classification of the employee based on the criteria: Advantage, Benefit and Ease of implementation.

When this suggestion enters the computer system, an alert is triggered for all employees to discuss it.

According to the rules established in the company, there is a deadline for everyone to make a decision, as indicated by the "Deadline" section, ensuring that there will be a concrete analytical decision making process over a time period, previously set.

Usually, compliance with the provision of advice has a mandatory character, so as to obtain the maximum efficiency of this tool.

Each employee will subsequently examine the suggestion, and they are able to modify it by adding their individual perspective in a constructive way, while also adding their "ranking" - the three main criteria – concerning the suggestion.

The field "root problem" (or opportunity), is an auxiliary for the top management, so they are able to perform an analysis of the suggestion, which is important to avoid implementation of two suggestions for solving the same problem, leaving these redundant.

Let's look at a practical example.

LOCAL _____ EP _____   DATE _04_ / _23_ / _2014_   TIME   _10: 30_
EMPLOYEE __José Rodrigues_____   FUNCTION _Driver_

Problem/Oportunity

_There are vehicles in circulation with expired insurance documents while the correct documentation is at _____
_company headquarters. If they are under investigation of the authorities, the company will be fined._____

Root problem? YES [ ]   NO [ ]

Base suggestion

I suggest you get a copy of the insurance green card and put it on the sun visor of vehicles so that each driver can
_always check the documentation when sitting behind the wheel, which is easier than checking official _____
_documents of cars everyday._____

Practical suggestion

_____
_____
_____

	1	2	3	4	5
Advantage			X		
Benefit					X
Easy implementation					X

Deadline for collecting opinions: _05_ / _23_ / _2014_
Completion date _____ : ___ / ___ / _____
Implementation date _____ : ___ / ___ / _____

Figure 77 - Focused simplification, form 1.1

José Rodrigues, who is a driver, identified a problem related to the lack of valid auto insurance documents aboard some of the company's trucks, meaning that the company is exposed to the possibility of being fined by the police for lack of proof of valid insurance.

It is known that the correct documents, within their validity, are at the company's headquarters, but it is necessary for someone to go to the office in advance to get the original documents and take them to the respective vehicle.

He made his proposal to prevent this problem from extending, once he understood that the greatest difficulty consists in the very fact that drivers do not have a clear perception of the expiry date of the documents that are in the trucks.

He identified a need for intervention, which will help increase the company's profitability, avoiding costs associated with lack of valid documentation in the event of an accident, or questioning (by law enforcement authorities), and feels that he is helping to improve the general situation of the company.

The next day, before the suggestion of José Rodrigues, the employee Diego Costa merely classified the suggestion based on the three main focus criteria.

LOCAL _____ EP _____ DATE _04_ / _24_ / _2014_ TIME ___16: 17__
EMPLOYEE __Diego Costa _____ FUNTION _Driver_

Problem/Oportunity
_There are vehicles in circulation with expired insurance documents while the correct documentation is at____
_company headquarters. If they are under investigation of the authorities, the company will be fined._____

Root problem? YES [ ]   NO [ ]

Base suggestion
I suggest you get a copy of the insurance green card and put it on the sun visor of vehicles so that each driver can
_always check the documentation when sitting behind the wheel, which is easier than checking the_____
car documents everyday.

Practical suggestion
_____
_____
_____

	1	2	3	4	5
Advantage					X
Benefit					X
Easy implementation					X

Deadline for collecting opinions: _05_ / _23_ / _2014_
Completion date _____ : ___/___/____
Implementation date _____ : ___/___/____

Figure 78 - Focused simplification, form 1.2

Diego Costa merely accepted the suggestion of his colleague. However, John Carter…

LOCAL _____ EP _____ DATE _04_ / _25_ / _2014_ TIME ___08: 00__
EMPLOYEE __John Carter _____ FUNCTION _Driver_

Problem/Oportunity
_There are vehicles in circulation with expired insurance documents while the correct documentation is at____
_company headquarters. Under investigation of the authorities the company will be fined._____

Root problem? YES [ ]   NO [ ]

Base suggestion
I suggest you get a copy of the insurance green card and put it on the sun visor of vehicles so that each driver can
always check the documentation when sitting behind the wheel, making it easier than checking everyday the
official documents of the cars.

Practical suggestion
I suggest you get a copy of the insurance green card and put it on the sun visor of vehicles so that each driver can
_always check the documentation when sitting behind the wheel, which is easier than checking the_____
car documents everyday.

	1	2	3	4	5
Advantage					X
Benefit					X
Easy implementation					X

Deadline for collecting opinions: _05_ / _23_ / _2014_
Completion date _____ : ___/___/____
Implementation date _____ : ___/___/____

Figure 79 - Focused simplification, form 1.3

John Carter made a practical suggestion for improvement of the original suggestion which was initially formulated by José Rodrigues.

Without facing strict limits of time, three employees have already stated their opinion, a possible solution for the problem, and a constructive proposal to improve the initial suggestion.

The creative process has now some space; it happens at the right time, without pressures, and has conditions to be closer to the actual potential of the organization.

When there are many practical suggestions, the person responsible for monitoring this process plays an active role, by choosing the suggestion that better serves the interest of the company.

The problem concerns all. The solution is also for everyone.

Let us see how it evolves by using a second practical example.

Louise Kenway, an official of the Sales Department of the bank "ABC", considered that the celebration of the World Cup in 2014 would be an opportunity for the bank that could be exploited.

She formalized her suggestion accordingly:

LOCAL _____ EP _____	DATE _11_ / _21_ / _2013_	TIME ____14: 18_
EMPLOYEE __Louise Kenway_____		FUNCTION _Sales D._

Problem/Oportunity

In 2014, the World Cup in Brazil provides us an opportunity to boost our brand awareness and taking something
out of the event.

Root problem? YES ☐   NO ☐

Base suggestion

For every 100,000 customers who make deposits in our bank between May, 01 and May,31 we'll give away a
trip for two people to watch the Fifa World Cup Final and closing ceremony in Brazil .
We promote the slogan: "It pays to be a customer at bank "ABC"!"

Practical suggestion

_____
_____
_____

	1	2	3	4	5
Advantage				X	
Benefit				X	
Easy implementation				X	

Deadline for collecting opinions: _12_ / _21_ / _2013_
Completion date _____ : ___ / ___ / ____
Implementation date _____ : ___ / ___ / ____

Figure 80 - Focused simplification, form 2.1

Tom Peters, from the marketing department, which is responsible for budgeting of such actions, felt that the idea of colleague Louise Kenway is good but, as it stands, lacks some practical applicability.

He has some difficulty with the budgeting of the project because the usual number of depositor customers, throughout the month, shows a remarkable statistical variance.

LOCAL _____ EP _____ DATE _11_ / _23_ / _2013_   TIME ___09: 48__
EMPLOYEE __Tom Peters_____   FUNCTION __Mkt Cs.

Problem/Oportunity

In 2014, the World Cup in Brazil provides us an opportunity to boost our brand awareness and taking something
out of the event.

Root problem? YES ☐   NO ☐

Base suggestion

For every 100,000 customers who make deposits in our bank between May, 01 and May,31 we'll give away a
trip for two people to watch the Fifa World Cup Final and closing ceremony in Brazil .
We promote the slogan: "It pays to be a customer at bank "ABC"!"

Practical suggestion

In May 2014, we'll have a weekly sweepstake among our customers to offer a trip for two people to go to Brazil
and attend the final of the Fifa World Cup / 2014 and its closing ceremony. Thus we can control the costs of
promotion knowing that we have to safeguard 4 trips.

	1	2	3	4	5
Advantage					X
Benefit			X		
Easy implementation					X

Deadline for collecting opinions: _05_ / _23_ / _2014_
Completion date _____ : ___ / ___ / _____
Implementation date _____ : ___ / ___ / _____

Figure 81 - Focused simplification, form 2.2

Tom Peters expressed his concern about the need for cost control and operationalization of the promotion. Louise Kenway identified the opportunity and suggested a promotion that would guarantee the "ABC" bank a financial return, materialized in the form of customer deposits.

Tom Peters's suggestion had practical objectivity, with the exact definition of the budget required for promotion. Since the need for customer deposits was revealed, the incentive to take an additional return from the promotion was lost.

While Louise Kenway assigns the ABE a (4,4,4) classification, Tom Peters considers ABE a (5,3,5).

Whenever a practical suggestion occurs over the original suggestion, the responsible for monitoring the "FS - Focused Simplification" process, will reset the original suggestion so it appears consolidated when submitted for rating by the remaining employees.

This action is important because it brings greater advantage from latent creativity in the company, providing a focused evolution in three fundamental aspects (Advantage, Benefit and Ease of implementation), without precipitating value judgments. Meanwhile, top management consolidates its own perceptions, keeping in mind different perspectives from employees who are discovering the same problem.

Managers reset the original suggestion, in order to seize the objective of raising deposits from customers, as recommended by Louise Kenway, and maintaining dominion over the project costs, as suggested by Tom Peters:

Base suggestion

In May/2014, from day 01 to 31,we will have a weekly raffle among our customers who'll make deposits in that
period. We'll give away a trip to Brazil for two people to attend the Fifa World Cup Final and closing ceremony.
Sweepstakes at May 09, 16, 23 and 31. "It pays to be a customer at bank "ABC"!"

Figure 82 - Focused simplification, modified base suggestion

The employee Anna Carmo, at Cityplace, has come across a different layout of the suggestion and so she participated in the process.

LOCAL	Cityplace	DATE 12 / 03 / 2013	TIME 16: 41
EMPLOYEE	Anna Carmo		FUNCTION Front O.

Problem/Oportunity

In 2014, the World Cup in Brazil provides us an opportunity to boost our brand awareness and taking something out of the event.

Root problem? YES ☐ NO ☐

Base suggestion

In May/2014, from day 01 to 31, we will have a weekly raffle among our customers who'll make deposits in that period. We'll give away a trip to Brazil for two people to attend the Fifa World Cup Final and closing ceremony. Sweepstakes at May 09, 16, 23 and 31. "It pays to be a customer at bank "ABC"!"

Practical suggestion

	1	2	3	4	5
Advantage					X
Benefit					X
Easy implementation					X

Deadline for collecting opinions: 05 / 23 / 2014
Completion date _____ : ___ / ___ / _____
Implementation date _____ : ___ / ___ / _____

Figure 83 - Focused simplification, form 2.3

Anna Carmo understood she had nothing to add to the original suggestion, now under consideration, and merely classified the suggestion.

Although it does not appear so, it is extremely important to collect this information.

For Anna Carmo, the idea is extremely advantageous, beneficial and easy to implement.

If the large majority of employees have this same feeling and top management concludes that it is not feasible, it is necessary to explain to employees why it is unfeasible.

Thus, top management demonstrates its respect for the opinion of people who constitute the organization, valuing their participation, and expressing what are the real needs of the organization.

If the overall rating of a suggestion is not positive, all employees naturally accept that the suggestion is not viable.

To conclude, we have to collect the classification of all employees of the company (or a large majority - for example: 90.0% - where it becomes impossible to ensure the participation of all in due time, when companies are too big), and aggregate their evaluations.

For instance, for a company with ten workers, ABE ratings of a particular suggestion could be as follows:

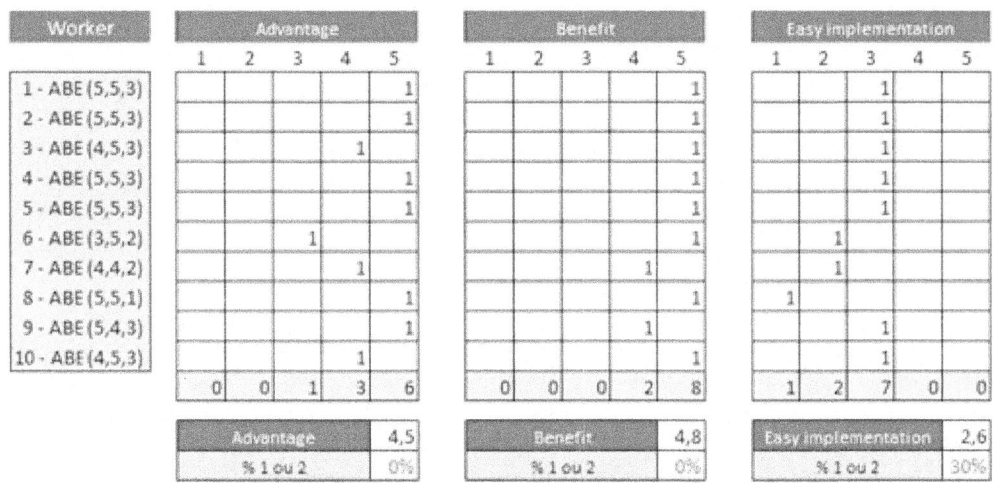

Figure 84 - Focused simplification, ABE calculations

Advantage = (1 x 0/10) + (2 x 0/10) + (3 x 1/10) + (4 x 3/10) + (5 x 6/10)
Benefit = (1 x 0/10) + (2 x 0/10) + (3 x 0/10) + (4 x 2/10) + (5 x 8/10)
Ease of implementation = (1 x 1/10) + (2 x 2/10) + (3 x 7/10) + (4 x 0/10) + (5 x 0/10)
% 1 or 2 (Advantage) = (0+0)/10
% 1 or 2 (Benefit) = (0+0)/10
% 1 or 2 (Easy Implementation) = (1+2)/10

In this example, the suggestion's final classification would be ABE (4.5; 4.8; 2.6).

The ranges of values, which validate a suggestion, depend on what is defined by the company as "minimum accepted values."

The company may define that, for values 1 and 2, 20.0% or higher percentages in any of the evaluation criteria will prevent the implementation of that suggestion.

For instance, the company can also set a global rating higher than "4" in the three main criteria as being necessary, so that we can validate the implementation of the suggestion.

As a result, the fourth step of the methodology concerns the definition of the terms of implementation by setting it on the "Table of Activities" (see p. 25), i.e., defining how it will be implemented, who will implement, with what resources and when it will be implemented.

Table of Activities

Measures	Responsable	Participants	Time	Costs	Schedule
Measure 1	xyz	...		1500	Set - Nov
Action 1	jyk	...	2 h		Set
Action 2	qwe	...	2 h		Oct
Measure 2	xyz	...		2000	Set - Dec
Action 1	abc	...	3 h		Nov
...	...	...			

Figure 85 - Focused simplification, Table of activities

The fifth and final step of the methodology is adequate disclosure regarding the process, whether in the case of implementation, or in the case of non-implementation.

Summing up the methodology step by step, it is as follows:

1º   Assume that any suggestion should be implemented;
2º   Create an expeditious process of collecting and processing suggestions;
3º   Submit a suggestion for analysis with objectivity and support on three basic criteria: advantage, benefit and ease of implementation;
4º   Quickly finish the terms of implementation of the suggestion by setting its "Table of Activities";
5º   Properly disclose conclusions about the process, in both cases: in the case of implementation and in the case of non-implementation.

We have an engaging, integrative process, for all elements of the organization. The freedom granted to any employee who wishes to express an opinion or a suggestion, for any area within the organization, makes that the simplest things that usually escape the eyes of those responsible, may be seen. This is useful both when solving problems and when seizing opportunities.

In this context, people mostly guide their thoughts towards simplification.

With the use of IT tools, generating ideas within the company is very practical, fast and focused.

This process allows further processing of a wide range of suggestions, for understanding several organizational aspects:

- Where are the difficulties presented (most often);
- Identifying where are the opportunities, with more frequency;
- Identifying the areas of the company where there is major development potential;
- From what areas of the company are suggestions largely arising, and in which platform are they standing: difficulties or opportunities?

Implementation

For an effective implementation of this process, the company surely needs to go through the IT tools.

With the popularization of spreadsheets and e-mail boxes, you can define a set of rules and procedures that implement the FS process (FS - Focused Simplification).

What is ideal is that, when possible, this is done through the creation of computer program software that allows further support and management of the emerging information from this process. We are already observing some companies doing this.

This way, the top management of the company can further enrich the quality of their decisions.

Maintenance

The maintenance of the FS-Focused Simplification process involves a close connection with the SIS- Structured Information Support process.

As we have seen, the quality and effectiveness of the FS-Focused Simplification process depends on the existence and enforcement of rules by employees who require their own involvement in the assessment of suggestions, in a given period of time (one month in the previous examples). Maintenance also requires the careful and responsible implementation of the suggestions, since it defines who is responsible to do what, throughout the process.

Stiffness and professionalism must exist in the company, and both will be specifically required for the maintenance of the FS process.

Conclusion

With the "Focused Simplification" process, the result of personal involvement towards continuous improvement and the absence of negative criticism, will both help employees feel that they belong to the organization. This will in turn lead to confidence, now and in the future. Moreover, the company is now structured in a way that it boosts creativity. These feelings develop into a positive state of mind, that is exhorted even outside of the organization and is the foundation of a consistent excellent performance, over time.

This method values the minority. It appreciates everybody, including those who think differently, but also have good ideas. And good ideas are not to waste!

It fosters communication within the company through constructive debate concerning the suggestions under consideration.

It builds up a real sense of unity and purpose, when mutual aid is needed for implementation of certain actions.

Change is going to be to be a constant, accepted and based on the inherent stability to trusted relationships, assuring the organization's soundness.

Afterwards, check where your company is located...

	Focused Simplification				
Level 5: Continuously improve	Whether providing suggestions or through the ensuing debate, both are generalized to the whole organization and constructively sharpen individual creativity and collective progress.	The complementarity of individual capabilities emerges as the driving spring in the presentation of suggestions in the simplification process and creative liberation.	Validation criteria of the suggestions are subject to periodic review in the light of efficiency recorded in the past, ensuring focus on efficiency criteria.	Whenever a simplification suggestion is rejected or validated, the underlying criteria are appropriately disclosed, explained and understood.	The company is in constant search for efficient improvement, being attentive to the needs of adjustment in the methodology of the FS process.
Level 4: Focus on reliability	Communication is encouraged within the company, often resulting in significant improvements in the initial suggestion.	There is a growing resignation of individual position for the benefit of the collective; the various positions being based mainly in the spirit of the organization.	The validation or rejection of suggestions doesn't depend on the individual perspective of an employee and there is respect and appreciation of minority opinions.	The processes of collection and treatment suggestions are expeditious and processing times are known, respected and effective.	There is an effective control over the methodology applied in the treatment of the suggestions being guaranteed an adequate dosing flow of suggestions within the organization.
Level 3: Make it visual	A suggestions' management support of easy and widespread access query is created, being encouraged to use to promote the release of creativity.	It can be noted the widespread acceptance of the suggestions without the manifest of judgements of negative critical value. The suggestions are subject to constructive debate within the company.	The validation process of suggestions is perceived without a deeper need to explain why a validation or rejection occurs.	Unimplemented suggestions do not constitute a source of dissatisfaction for any member of the company. Everyone is proud of the suggestions that were implemented.	The methodology applied in the treatment of suggestions is clearly defined in information support, duly publicized and it is easy to use by any organization member.
Level 2: Focus on basics	Suggestions are submitted to debate in the company, promoting the involvement of everyone, even those who do not reap direct effects of a given suggestion.	The company encourages dissenting opinions, aware that individual creativity should enhance collective development.	The analysis of the suggestions is comprehensive and based on practical criteria and objectives, facilitating the decision (validation or rejection) for different perspectives.	Any suggestion is worthy of the same treatment regardless of their origin, taking advantage of economies of experience.	The principles and steps involved in the methodology of collection, analysis, validation and implementation of the suggestions are defined.
Level 1: Just starting	The submission of suggestions to the direction of the company by workers is ephemeral or nonexistent. When it comes up, the suggestion is not the subject of debate within the company.	In general, it is assumed in the company that what is determined by the top management is right and each one has only the function of assisting the execution of what is defined.	The analysis of the suggestions is concentrated in little more than a person, and the decision to implement is skewed by their individual perspective.	Suggestions are implemented or rejected without proper attention to who made the suggestion, without taking advantage of economies of experience.	There is not a methodology for collecting, analyzing and validating the suggestions. The implementation respects only the rules of the department where it applies to.
Place yellow box where each area is on the FS Levels of Achievement	**Participation**	**Respect for Differences**	**Objectivity**	**Suggestions treatment**	**Methodology**

Figure 86 - Focused simplification levels

3.0 CONCLUSION

Dynamics, tone and resonance are key concepts in an organization's life.

So it concerns to enterprise purposes, organization, execution, human relationships, emotions and feelings that emerge there, buzzing and consolidating over time.

Dynamics, tone and resonance give meaning to an organization.

Execution levels depend on the dynamics of the company's structure. The tone with which things are done, with more or less color, sound, or intensity will definitely affect the final result.

The resonance that each organization can give to the events that might affect it, whether positive or negative, will certainly determine the company's ability to be its own first determinant element of success.

The culture of an organization is always closely linked to these three concepts, and is unique in each working group.

Managing a Team, as herein defined, among their rational and emotional spheres, should enhance the dynamics, tone and resonance of the actions of the organization, in a positive context.

Each organization has its own idiosyncrasies in three basic levels of analysis: skills, processes and people.

These features define a potential, which must be used in full.

Build and consolidate your Team.

Build up the "SIS - Structured Information Support", to align behaviors, facilitate communication and ensure effectiveness.

The process of "FS - Focused Simplification" is built to create conditions for Excellency, joining the team and turning it into a diamond that exudes objective creativity, which benefits everyone.

When the changes are made in a process of co-consultancy with the staff, everything becomes easier. There is less resistance to change and a higher propensity to collaborate in implementing changes.

Things change with stability!

Grounded in the concepts of Team, Structured Information Support and Focused Simplification, the direction of any organization is able to evolve in a controlled way, safely, and with the confidence needed to create healthy and positive environments, both individual and collective.

What is good management?

The management is detailed in four functions: planning, organizing, directing and motivating.

The functions of management have a sequential effectiveness, the next one depending directly on the quality that their predecessors have shown, during their execution in the organization.

Otherwise, the consistency of the organization's success will be compromised.

Managing is different from controlling.

Figure 87 - Managing vs Controlling

Controlling is an action that is contained in the broader actions of planning, organizing, directing and motivating, but these are not exhausted in the control processes.

It is the quality of the management that is relevant!

Throughout this book, the topic of management was addressed in general and organizational behavior in particular. This book is an introduction to an important set of concepts, which are helpful if they are explored thoroughly, to bring forth their full potential.

It has the merit of helping managers to link the major generic concepts inherent to an organization, and the importance of coordination between the rational and emotional spheres for the success of any team.

Hopefully, it will deepen your management knowledge, by prioritizing the issues that will create the highest levels of effectiveness to you.

Technically, the rational aspects of a company in terms of strategy, structure and execution, can be enhanced detail to detail, far beyond what is explained here.

The same applies to the emotional aspects of the company, in terms of Communication, Commitment and Mutual Aid.

What is particularly relevant is the simplicity with which any organization can very quickly identify the points of strength and weakness by way of these perspectives, and identify where there is a need to take action.

The greater the control over the rational and emotional spheres and their relationship within the company, the greater the objectivity of your team's actions as herein defined, that are consolidated by taking care of the individual and the collective interests, ideas and beliefs, between the lines of convergent and divergent thinking.

The existence of a physical support for information that clearly defines the limits and action guidelines throughout the organization is crucial to ensure operation in unison.

The exploitation of individual economies of experience, that comprise the organization, is the extreme step which allows a more distinctive position against the competition to be obtained.

An organization that can do their day-to-day activities in collective terms will never depend on the level of performance of a single employee. Employees who join a company where their professional growth is continuous, will always feel less tempted to look for another employer.

Excellence is achieved when individual creativity is put to the service of the organization, surprising positively.

Success is only complete when it is both individual and collective!

"Simplicity is the ultimate sophistication."

Leonardo Da Vinci

APPENDIX

Team
SIS – Structured Information Support
FS – Focused Simplification

Team
    Rational
    Emotional

SIS – Structured Information Support
    Principles
    Method

FS – Focused Simplification
    Principles
    Method

Team
    Rational
        Strategy
        Structure
        Execution

    Emotional
        Commmunication
        Commitment
        Mutual Aid

SIS – Structured Information Suport
    Principles
        Convergence and Unity
        Safety and trust

    Method
        Identifying needs
        Understanding actions
        Standardizing practices
        Managing contingencies

FS – Focused Simplification
    Principles
        Curiosity and Involvement
        Dynamics and Efficiency

    Method
        Assume that any suggestion should be implemented
        Create an expeditious process of collecting and processing suggestions
        Surrounding classification of suggestions based on three basic criteria:
            advantage, benefit and easy implementation
        Quickly finish the terms of implementation of the suggestion,
            setting its "Table of Activities"
        Properly disclose conclusions about the process

Team
    Rational
        Strategy
            Who are we?
            What do we want to achieve?
            What's the situation?
            What's our plan?

        Structure
            Components
            Degree of freedom
            Soundness

        Execution
            Alignment
            Monitoring
            Results
            Mistakes

    Emotional
        Communication
            Good faith, respect, dignity
            Sharing, Dialogue
            Ability for listening, for conducting a constructive debate, to find joint solutions
            Expression - Interpretation - Understanding

        Commitment
            Complacency, indifference, lack of motivation
            Joy
            Meaning, purpose
            Intensity, focus, objectivity

        Mutual Aid
            Common goals
            Trust, gratitude
            Complexity of hierarchical structures

SIS – Structured Information Suport
    Advantages
        Adaptability of training needs
        Cost reduction
        Productivity increase
        Communication gains

FS – Focused Simplification
    Advantages
        Cost reduction
        Greater operational efficiency
        Greater capacity for innovation
        Higher level of excellence (greater capacity to surprise positively)

    Challenges
        Integration and involvement of all
        Appreciate the suggestions with objectivity, respect for differences and without making value judgments
        Ensure that unimplemented suggestions cause no problems
        Developing a methodology

ABOUT THE AUTHOR

José Rodrigues, has a degree in Economics by Universidade Nova de Lisboa.

He has an extense and diversified professional experience, and was connected to Banco Nacional Ultramarino SA, Auto Viação Micaelense Lda, Corretora Fincor – Açores, Ponta Delgada Professional Vocational School, Insurance Company Mundial Confiança SA and Insurance Company Fidelidade SA.

For three years he was responsible for Economics page of the weekly newspaper "Expresso das Nove", published in Azores (Portugal).

At the moment, he's connected to Allianz.

This professional experience allowed for the sum of experiences as team manager, coach and several times participant in constructive debate environments, in order to find precise solutions.

He is particular keen of the organizational structure dynamics and its multidisciplinary impact on what's around: people, brand and competition.

He believes that structuring a company to exploit creativity of those who's related with, is a must to ensure an overwhelming competitive power.

José Rodrigues, 2014

TABLE OF FIGURES

www.ingramcontent.com/pod-product-compliance
Lightning Source LLC
Chambersburg PA
CBHW080300180526

45167CB00006B/2602